No Big Deal!

Mastering the Art of Miniature Quiltmaking

I think no virtue
goes with size.

Ralph Waldo Emerson
The Titmouse

That Patchwork Place®

Deborah L. White

Dedication

FLEETING THOUGHT

I glimpse my children who grin no care

I whiff of spring no longer there

Vapors of youthful intensities

How has such sweet life fled from me?
—Bob White, 1985

To David, Cheri, and Joey,
who are my whiffs of spring.

Acknowledgments

Many hugs and kisses to Joyce Becker, who is always my friend and who didn't give me a moment's rest until this book became a reality. Her help and encouragement continue to spark me on.

Special thanks to Elaine Earl, Mary Berdan, and Deborah Johnsen, students who rose to the challenge and, in the process, became my friends.

To Patti Cunningham, whose creativity I am always in awe of, and who finally gave in and quilted one of the quilts for me. It is an honor.

To Bob, who always keeps my computer running and drives me in ways he doesn't even know.

To Sally Schneider and That Patchwork Place, for making me feel at home among the experts. Sally shared her bias-square method without even a blink!

Always good for a smile, Gerry Kimmel-Carr and Red Wagon Designs are a constant delight and the inspiration behind "An Angel to Watch Over Me."

Special hugs and kisses to my Grandma Dziuk, who taught me the thrill of creating something with my hands and started a lifelong creative journey.

Above all else, thank you to the Lord and creator of all things, for being generous enough to instill his creative nature in us all.

Library of Congress Cataloging-in-Publication Data
White, Deborah L.
     No big deal : mastering the art of miniature quiltmaking / by Deborah L. White.
       p. cm.
     ISBN 1-56477-183-0
     1. Patchwork—Patterns. 2. Quilting—Patterns. 3. Miniature quilts. I. Title.
TT835.W494 1997
746.46'041—dc21   96-49186
                                          CIP

Credits

Editor-in-Chief	Kerry I. Smith
Technical Editor	Sally Schneider
Managing Editor	Judy Petry
Copy Editor	Tina Cook
Proofreaders	Melissa Riesland, Leslie Phillips
Design Director	Cheryl Stevenson
Cover Designer	Sandy Wing
Text Designer	Kay Green
Production Assistant	Marijane E. Figg
Illustrator	Laurel Strand
Photographer	Brent Kane

No Big Deal:
Mastering the Art of Miniature Quiltmaking
©1997 by Deborah L. White

That Patchwork Place, Inc., PO Box 118
Bothell, WA 98041-0118 USA

Printed in the United States of America
02 01 00 99 98 97   6 5 4 3 2

MISSION STATEMENT

We are dedicated to providing quality products and service by working together to inspire creativity and to enrich the lives we touch.

TABLE OF CONTENTS

PREFACE

Life is uncertain, especially when it comes to your gene pool. You never know what quirk you might have picked up from your ancestors.

People often ask me why I do miniatures. I know the question is coming, and I feel a little smirk forming as I reply, "I like little and I like intricate, and I do these crazy, insane things with fabric because there is a glitch in my gene pool."

I didn't realize just how accurate this statement was until I visited my grandmother and had an "under the quilt" experience. On the bed there was a Trip Around the World quilt that Grammy, my great-grandmother, had hand pieced using one-inch squares. I lay in bed with the lamp on, counting the squares and hoping my husband wouldn't wake up and catch me. Sixty-seven rows across by eighty-one rows down—there were 5,427 one-inch squares in Grammy's

Mona Grace Walbeck
"Grammy"
1886–1973

quilt. As I looked at the fabrics, I realized that she had fussy-cut each square: the stripes ran the same way in each block, every flower was centered, every seam matched perfectly. I lay there that night, teary eyed, communing with a quilt!

Grammy was a woman after my own heart. I, too, have been accused of being fussy when it comes to cutting: every stripe runs the same way and flowers are centered just right. Perfectionism runs through my veins.

I spent many moments wrapped in the experience of Grammy's quilt, knowing I had just discovered a part of my being. Now, when I am asked why I do miniatures, I think about Grammy fussy cutting more than five thousand one-inch squares and I feel a part of her in me as I reply with pride, "It's because of a glitch in my gene pool!"

INTRODUCTION

I used to approach a new miniature-quilt design as though I were preparing for battle. Will I be able to accomplish this design, or will it get me in the end?

If you have ever tried to make a miniature quilt, perhaps you know what I mean. Some of us make one miniature quilt and are never the same again. The tiny pieces and the challenge of attempting the seemingly impossible capture our hearts and never let go.

Other quilters, however, do not get caught up in the passion. This became apparent to me one night when I spoke at a local quilt guild. One of the guild members raised her hand to ask if she could share her miniature quilt with me. Throughout the evening I had noticed a sly smile on her lips and wondered what she was up to. I watched as she took out an envelope, dumped a pile of little pieces onto the table, and proclaimed that it was her first and last attempt at making a miniature quilt. This brought laughter from the other guild members, but it made me aware that there is a great need for good, workable techniques in this area of quilt art.

Some people, like me, have become obsessed with making miniature quilts. I attack a new design with determination and zeal, teeth grinding and fabric flying. My family flees when they see the crazed look in my eyes. They breathe a sigh of relief as the fabric pieces finally settle and I contentedly sew the last few stitches into the binding. As peace settles over the household and my family begins to relax, a new miniature-quilt idea inevitably starts to take shape, and the fun begins again.

Each time I launch into a new design, my goal is to develop techniques that make miniature quiltmaking easier, rather than just fanatically striving for a product. When I began making miniature quilts, I religiously followed the "rules of quilting," but it soon became apparent that miniature-quilt makers needed a whole new set of guidelines.

Over the past ten years, I've developed and adapted methods that eliminate some problems associated with making miniature quilts. In this book, you will learn a variety of techniques, such as how to ensure accurate ⅛"-wide seam allowances, how to piece with freezer-paper templates to stabilize bias edges, and how to make your miniature quilt come alive with pieced and appliquéd borders. The projects give you the opportunity to create a simple treasure or an heirloom-quality showpiece.

I have often heard, "How does she do that?" This is how: I love solving the problems that come with making quilts with tiny pieces. Now the challenge is yours. Learn to work through problems, and enjoy the process while creating intricate quilts. Using the designs and techniques provided, you too can become a master of the art of miniature-quiltmaking. Enjoy yourself.

Deborah

Grammy made this quilt in Leland, Idaho, in 1938 as a wedding quilt for my grandparents, Bill and Florence Dziuk.

EQUIPMENT

TEAR-AWAY BACKING: Stitching on a foundation is the secret to success in miniature quiltmaking, and I use tear-away backing for this purpose. There are several brands on the market, such as Pellon® Stitch-n-Tear and Easy Stitch™ Tear Away. These products are available in the interfacing section of any fabric store. I prefer Stitch-n-Tear because it tears easily and doesn't leave residue in the seam allowance.

SEAM RIPPER: The seam ripper is my friend. It is an extended finger that guides the fabric through the sewing machine as well as being a "reverse sewer." The smaller seam rippers work best for removing the tiny stitches used in miniature quiltmaking.

TWEEZERS: Tweezers are useful for removing paper foundations and for picking up micro-mini pieces.

MASKING TAPE: I use ¾"-wide masking tape to build seam guides on sewing machines. Spongy seam guides tend to wear down, allowing the seam allowance to grow. Masking tape is readily available and doesn't wear down.

ROTARY CUTTER: The regular large-blade cutter works best. I have two cutters, one for template plastic and one for fabric.

CUTTING MATS: My little 5½" x 8½" gem goes with me everywhere. It sits by my sewing machine and gets packed in my goody bag when I travel. The small size means you can rotate the mat instead of walking around it. The 11" x 17" size is good for quick cutting jobs, and it is easy to grab and doesn't take up much space. The 17" x 23" mat is best when you have a lot of strips to cut.

RULERS: Those with ⅛" increments are essential. A 3" x 18" or 3" x 12" ruler with a ⅛" grid is good for cutting strips and trimming edges. A 4" x 4" ruler with a ⅛" grid and a diagonal line, such as the Bias Square®, is the one I use most. It is easy to manipulate and handy for quick snips and squaring-up pieces. It is also essential for constructing bias squares.

FINE PINS: The Tru Point™ #17 is my favorite. Use small silk or bead pins for miniature appliqué.

APPLIQUÉ NEEDLES: Both the John James #11 and #12 Sharps and Richard Hemming™ #10 Milliners Needles are flexible and work well. The Richard Hemming Milliners are longer and have a larger eye for threading.

CHALK MARKER: I prefer the Chakoner™. Filled with blue chalk, it will mark both dark and light fabrics.

GLUESTICK: Glue is a good substitute for pins, which can distort and shift fabric. You can also use glue to temporarily hold appliqué pieces in place. Be safe; use a water-soluble gluestick made for fabric.

SEAM SEALANT: Sealants, such as FrayCheck™, come in handy for concave points in appliqué and for seam allowances that have shrunk to nothing. Test it first because it sometimes darkens fabric where it is applied.

SPRAY SIZING: Use it to add body and stability to washed fabric, especially when using the more loosely woven fabrics, such as some woven plaids.

MECHANICAL PENCIL: For drafting and making templates, a mechanical pencil with .05mm lead gives the finest line. Especially in miniature quiltmaking, a wide pencil line can adversely affect accuracy.

BLACK PERMANENT-INK PEN: The Sanford® Sharpie® Ultra Fine Point permanent marker has the thinnest line I've found and doesn't smudge easily. Use it to draw templates on plastic or to trace foundations.

FREEZER PAPER: Use it to make templates for piecing and appliqué. One roll will last a long time.

TRACING PAPER: Use it for foundation paper piecing.

TEMPLATE MATERIAL: A 10" x 10" square of template plastic is enough to make templates for all the quilts in this book.

FLANNEL BOARD: A flannel board helps you keep track of tiny pieces and doubles as a design board. To construct a homemade board, buy a self-stick needlework mounting board from your local craft store or frame shop. Cut a piece of flannel the same size as the board, and press it to the adhesive on the board. I use an 11" x 14" board; it's portable and fits easily beside my sewing machine.

RESEALABLE PLASTIC BAGGIES: Use the gallon size to store entire projects and the sandwich size to store individual pieces and blocks.

Iron: An iron with a pointed tip is best.

Tip

I pick up old steel-bottomed irons inexpensively at thrift stores and garage sales. (The black-handled General Electric irons are my favorites.) Your iron needs to be hot in order for freezer-paper templates to adhere to fabric, and older irons generally get hotter (and steam better) than newer models. They also have the pointed tips that are useful for ironing small pieces and pressing open seam allowances.

Wooden Bread Board: Freezer-paper templates stick best to fabric when pressed on a hard surface. Cover the board with a towel.

Sewing Machine: You need a machine that sews a good straight stitch and has an even, balanced tension. It helps to have a straight-stitch throat plate. Most machines come with a zigzag plate, but you might be able to purchase a separate straight-stitch plate with a small hole just large enough for a needle. The hole in the zigzag plate tends to suck in ⅛"-wide seam allowances. There is also a straight-stitch foot available for most machines. This foot is narrow, which makes it easier to see small pieces.

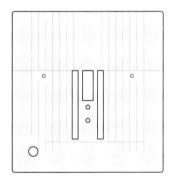

Straight-Stitch Plate

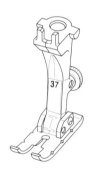

Straight-Stitch Foot

If your machine has a detachable platform, be sure to use it. It supports your fabric in front of the machine.

#70 Sharp Machine Needles: Finer needles make smaller holes and are therefore more appropriate for miniatures.

Thread: You can use regular-weight threads successfully, but fine-weight threads blend into fabric better. Try 100% cotton lingerie threads or extra-fine machine-embroidery threads.

Thread color is always a challenge, especially if you are using high-contrast fabrics. In my experience, dark thread shows more on light fabrics than light thread does on dark fabrics. If you have a piece that has a lot of lights and darks coming together, use a light, neutral thread.

Chocolate: Chocolate and quilting, quilting and chocolate. What more can I say? This is a must on every supply list.

Tip

I have a selection of permanent Pigma™ pens that I use in sticky situations. When I'm chain piecing and two dark fabrics come together after a light fabric, I don't change threads; I continue with the light thread. After the piece is sewn, I open the seam allowance and dot the light threads with a black or coordinating-color Pigma pen. Don't try this on anything but 100% cotton fabric or thread; the ink will bleed through the fibers of blends.

FABRIC

Good color sense comes easily for some, but for others, it's like a petal floating on the wind—you can see it but can't seem to catch it. There are numerous books about color theory, but in the end you will use the colors that please you. What you like and don't like is inherent—it's a gene thing.

I use two different color styles in my quilts. I prefer muted colors on my walls, but I use bright, eye-catching colors in the quilts I make for competition. My first quilt instructor wanted me to use colors that moved. I had two toddlers at the time, and as far as I was concerned, I had enough things moving around me without my walls moving too. I love bright colors, but I have a hard time living with them on a consistent basis.

Play with the colors in your fabric collection and find your own color sense. If you like the colors in an existing quilt, then make another one like it! Soon you will begin to see things that you would like to change, and your personal color style will begin to emerge. Keep your fabrics out where your eyes can feast on them and your mind can play with them. Eventually your color combinations will begin to reflect your personality.

Texture plays a big part in the eye-catching appeal of your quilt. Texture is the design printed on or woven into the fabric. It is felt with your eyes, not with your hands. The color may be right, but the texture may leave a quilt flat. Mix stripes and florals with plaids and geometrics; add some pin dots and paisleys. The texture of the fabric adds to the charm of the quilt.

Part of the fun of miniature quiltmaking is finding a fabric that works. Look for small-scale prints, but don't overlook larger prints that have a special little design that you can fussy cut. A star or flower in just the right spot will be an attention-getter. Look for fabrics that have a motif you like, and plan your miniature around it.

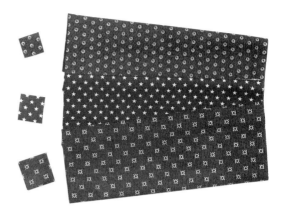

Throw in a little bit of plaid, a little bit of paisley, and some stripes and you'll have a feast for the eyes.

To avoid fraying, always use tightly woven, 100% cotton fabric. Fraying causes seam allowances to disappear. Most plaids and stripes are notorious for fraying, but I can't live without them. A little spray sizing will help stabilize your fabric. Don't overlook stripes and plaids for appliqué; they give it an added charm.

The smaller the pieces, the less color definition and contrast there will be. If you are planning a micro-mini quilt, the color contrast must be high or the pattern will be lost. Fabric with a lot of pattern will lose color definition when cut for miniatures. Some lines of fabric are made specifically for miniatures. Use them in small quantities, and mix the lines of fabric for a more individual look. Don't discount the pleasure of the hunt and the challenge of digging through bolts to find that perfect piece of fabric.

MINIATURE QUILTS

Is it a pot holder or a work of art? I believe every miniature-quilt artist has had to deal with this problem. Avoiding dimensions that might look like pot holders, place mats, or pillows eliminates some confusion. Make your miniature quilt a complete representation of a full-size quilt; it should look like a full-size quilt, only smaller. This applies to the design of the quilt top and the number of blocks, as well as to the quilting design.

Treat your miniatures as works of art; display them as you would paintings, placing them in groupings on the wall with other decorations.

Miniature-quilt standards vary from region to region, but consider 4"-square blocks and 24" per side as maximums. My personal maximums are 3" blocks and 18" per side. (I have broken this rule a few times when necessary.) These sizes give me the challenge I crave and keep the intricate look that is the charm of the miniature quilt.

In this day and age of quick and easy, anything time-consuming is often mistaken as being difficult. Many intricate designs have steps that, in themselves, are simple. The combination of many simple steps often makes a quilt appear difficult. Keep this in mind when you look at a project. You might be surprised once you understand the pattern dynamics.

A new technique or pattern sometimes seems difficult just because it is unfamiliar. Remember that the first block is always the hardest. You are learning; be patient.

BASIC TECHNIQUES

My motto for miniature quiltmaking is, "Whatever works!" If what you are doing works, keep doing it. I developed the following techniques through trial and error—and sometimes serendipity—and they are crucial to the success of your miniature quilt. Other techniques specific to individual patterns are included with that pattern (although these techniques are also useful for all miniature quiltmaking).

Whatever techniques you use, remember that accuracy is the key—it will make or break your miniature. The smaller the scale, the greater the need for accuracy. A discrepancy of ⅛" in a large quilt is not a big deal, but in a miniature it can be deadly. I stress accuracy and the ways to achieve it throughout this book.

NOTE: At the end of each pattern is a section called "Potential Problems and How to Solve Them." These are drawn from student or personal experience. Read these sections before you begin your quilt so you can avoid the problems described. Some problems have no practical explanation; these I call "fabric flukes," meaning the fabric has a mind of its own and there's no way to fix it. We have all run into the fabric demon from time to time.

MEASURING SEAM ALLOWANCES

I use ⅛"-wide seam allowances for most of my quilts. Just the mention of ⅛"-wide seam allowance strikes fear in the hearts of quiltmakers, but ¼"-wide seams are too bulky for miniature quilts. Occasionally, I use ¼"-wide seams on the outer edges of the blocks if there are a lot of points to match. (See "Blackjack" on page 74.)

1. Set your stitch length to 12 to 15 stitches per inch. If your sewing machine has numbers and not actual stitch lengths, set your stitch a little smaller than usual but not so small that you can't rip it out.

2. Stack six 5"-long pieces of masking tape, one on top of the other, aligning the layers carefully. I prefer masking tape because it is always available and doesn't wear down like spongy seam guides.

3. Place the tape so it extends 1" beyond the back of the feed dogs and several inches in front. Mark the position of the feed dogs on the tape, and then cut a notch out of the tape so it does not hinder the movement of the feed dogs.

Place the 4" ruler under the presser foot, painted side up, and lower the needle gently onto the ⅛" mark. Making sure the ruler is straight, place the tape on the throat plate along the edge of the ruler, with the notched edge clearing the feed dogs.

4. To check for accuracy, sew a seam on scrap fabric and measure the seam allowance. Make adjustments if necessary.

PIECING WITH TEAR-AWAY BACKING

We've all started a seam only to watch the fabric disappear into the needle hole. To eliminate this fabric gobbler, I use tear-away backing, such as Stitch-n-Tear, as a foundation. The backing stabilizes the tiny fabric pieces and acts as a stitching guide, which increases your accuracy. *Tear-away backing is the most essential ingredient for success in miniature quiltmaking.* A straight-stitch throat plate also helps.

1. Cut a piece of Stitch-n-Tear large enough to accommodate the pieces to be stitched; 3" x 4" is a good size. Make sure the sides are straight.

2. Align the pieces to be stitched, right sides together, with the right edge of the Stitch-n-Tear. Pin in place.

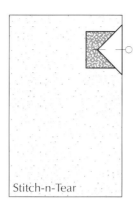

Stitch-n-Tear

NOTE: If pieces are shifting, or if you are making a micro-mini that pins would distort, baste with a gluestick. Apply the glue to the very edge of the seam allowance, being careful not to extend it beyond the stitching line.

3. Place the edge of the Stitch-n-Tear along the edge of the masking-tape guide (page 10) and sew; use your seam ripper to guide the pieces and keep them straight. You can also chain-piece on the Stitch-n-Tear.

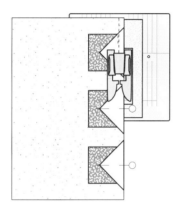

NOTE: Be sure to backstitch. Only a few stitches hold some of these tiny units together and any strain, such as tugging to match seams, can pop stitches. Removing the Stitch-n-Tear strains the stitches too; backstitching keeps them in place.

4. Remove the Stitch-n-Tear from the back of each piece by cutting a notch from the lower right toward the beginning of the stitching; hold the notched end, then quickly tear it up and over the seam allowance.

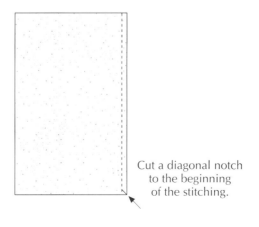

Cut a diagonal notch to the beginning of the stitching.

5. Trim the torn edges of the piece of Stitch-n-Tear, and then reuse it for the next seam.

NOTE: There is often a great deal of thread waste with miniature quilts. (I once used three spools on a single miniature.) To reduce waste, chain piece as much as possible, and begin and end with a lead-off scrap. The lead-off scrap will also help prevent the ugly stitches and tangled threads that some machines produce at the beginning of a seam. To make a lead-off scrap, fold a scrap of fabric in half and begin and end the stitching on it.

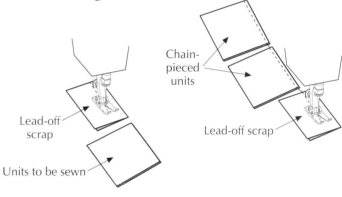

Chain-pieced units

Lead-off scrap

Units to be sewn

Lead-off scrap

PIECING WITH FREEZER-PAPER TEMPLATES

Freezer-paper templates act as cutting and stitching guides and also provide accurate points for pin matching. The greatest benefit of freezer paper, though, is that it stabilizes bias edges. Although each fabric piece needs its own freezer-paper template, I find the results are worth the time and effort.

1. Trace the full-size block onto the dull (uncoated) side of the freezer paper. Label the pieces as shown.

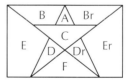

Full-size Star Block

NOTE: When you use freezer-paper piecing, the finished block is a mirror image of the drawn block. Keep this in mind if you make your own designs; asymmetrical designs come out the reverse of the paper design.

2. Using a rotary cutter and ruler, carefully cut the block apart on the lines.

3. Place the freezer-paper templates shiny side down on the wrong side of the fabric, allowing for ⅛"-wide seam allowances. Use a very hot iron (wool setting) and iron on a hard surface (page 7). Press the templates onto the fabric to the count of 10. Using a rotary cutter and ruler, cut out the pieces, adding a ⅛"-wide seam allowance. Leave the freezer paper attached.

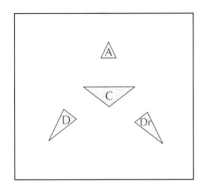

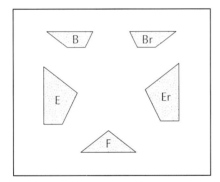

Freezer-paper templates on wrong side of fabric

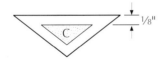

4. Place the first 2 pieces right sides together. Check to see that the points and seam lines are aligned by looking at them against a light source, or use a pin to match the points.
5. Using the paper edge as a seam guide, stitch the pieces together, stabilizing with Stitch-n-Tear.

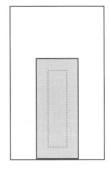

6. Remove the freezer paper when the block is complete.

PIECING WITH PAPER FOUNDATIONS

NOTE: The marked side of the paper foundation is the mirror image of the finished block. If your block is asymmetrical, it will appear as the reverse of the printed design.

1. Using any paper that will easily tear away after stitching (I prefer tracing paper), trace one foundation for each block in your quilt with a black permanent marker. Do not add the seam allowance around the outside edge; allow for it as you sew. If the seam allowance is included on the paper, you would have to pick it out with tweezers after sewing the seam. I haven't yet found anyone who gets a particular thrill out of this.

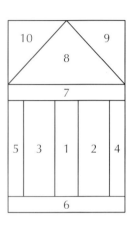

TIP

If you have a computer, try using your printer to produce paper foundations. The Electric Quilt, version 2.0 or 3.0, is especially valuable for drafting paper foundations.

2. On the unmarked side of the paper, place piece #1 right side up over space #1. Place piece #2 on piece #1, right sides together. Make sure fabric pieces extend beyond the seam lines. (Remember to allow for seam allowances on the outer edges.)

Unmarked side of paper

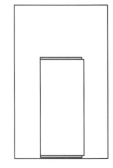

Fabric #1 over space #1

Fabric #2 right sides together with fabric #1

TIP

Dab a bit of gluestick on the back of piece #1 to keep it in place.

3. Set your stitch length to 12 to 15 stitches per inch. On the marked side, sew on the line between spaces #1 and #2. Trim seam allowances and finger-press piece #2 down before adding piece #3. Continue adding fabrics in the same manner, following the numerical sequence on the block.

Marked side of paper

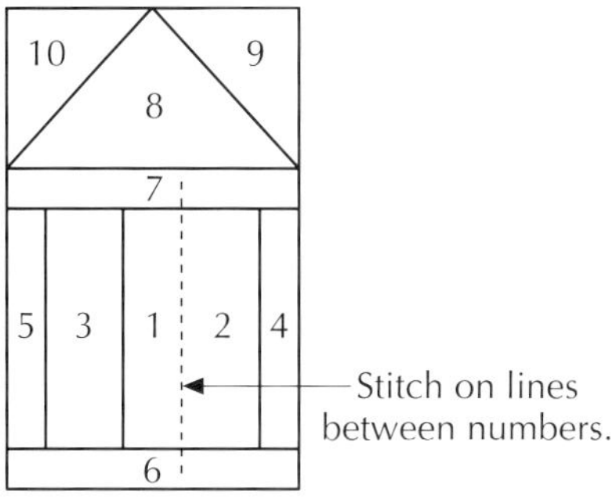

4. Trim each block, leaving a 1/8"-wide seam allowance around the outer edge. Do not remove the paper until after you have sewn the blocks into rows; the paper stabilizes the blocks and they go together more easily. Remove the paper before joining the rows.

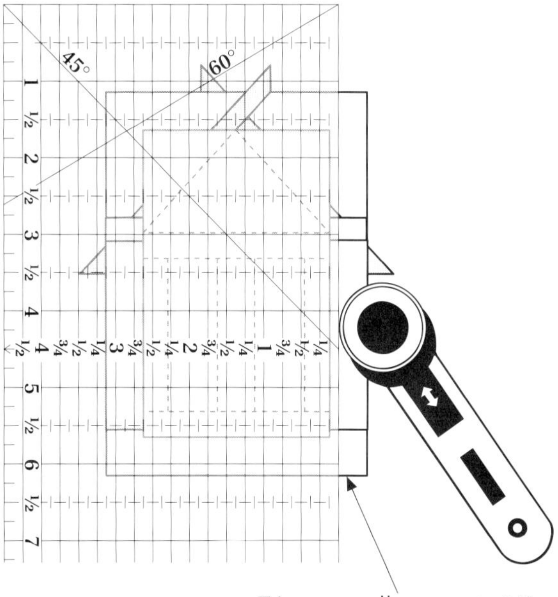

Trim seam allowance to 1/8".

Making Bias Squares

This method is convenient because there are no grids or math calculations, and you can make as many bias squares as you want. Cutting strips on the bias leaves the outer edges of the squares on the straight of grain.

Strip-Width Chart

Finished Size of Bias Square	Bias Strip Width	Cut Size of Bias Square
1/4"	5/8"	1/2"
3/8"	11/16"*	5/8"
1/2"	13/16"*	3/4"
5/8"	7/8"	7/8"
3/4"	15/16"*	1"
7/8"	17/16"*	1 1/8"
1"	1 1/8"	1 1/4"

*To measure 1/16", use a ruler with a 1/8" grid and eyeball the distance between two 1/8" marks, or mark the proper spot on your ruler with masking tape.

1. Determine the required *finished* size of the bias square; then add 1/4" to this measurement for seam allowances. For example, if the bias square is 3/4" finished, the cut size is 1", with 1/8"-wide seam allowances on all sides.
2. Referring to the chart above for the correct width, cut 2 bias strips, one light and one dark. Place the bias strips right sides together, then, using Stitch-n-Tear to stabilize the edges (page 10), sew along both long edges. Use a 1/8"-wide seam allowance. Press the strip flat.

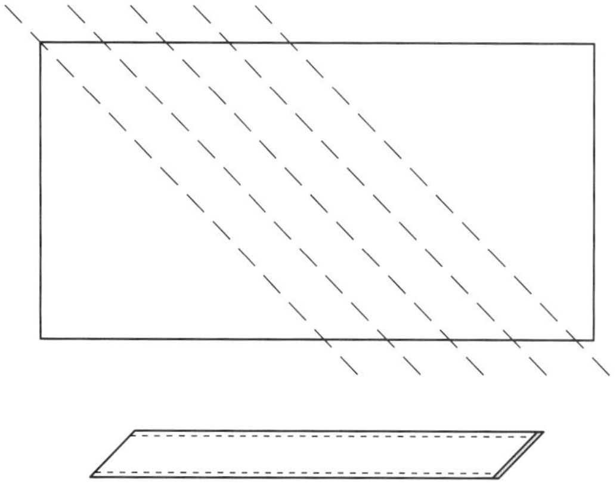

Stitch both sides.

3. Place the strip lengthwise on the cutting surface, with the pointed end on the left. (Reverse if you are left-handed.) Using a 4" Bias Square ruler, align the ruler's

diagonal line (45° angle) with the stitched seam as shown, and then trim the bottom end of the strip. Move the ruler so the diagonal line is on the stitched line and the desired cut size is on the cut edge. For example, if you want a 1" cut bias square, line up the 1" line with the fabric edge.

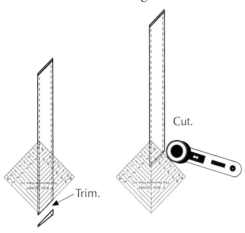

Cut.

Trim.

4. Turn the strip over and cut another bias square. If the edge of the ruler does not line up with the cut edge of the fabric, trim again.

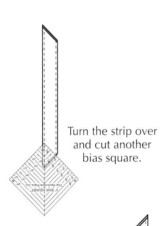

Turn the strip over and cut another bias square.

5. Continue to the end of the strip, turning the strip over after each cut.

6. Open each bias square and press the seam allowance toward the darker fabric.

7. To square up each bias square, place the diagonal line of the ruler on the diagonal seam of the bias square and trim if needed.

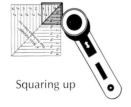

Squaring up

TIP

To calculate the strip width for any size bias square, draw the finished-size bias square onto a piece of graph paper. Add a ⅛"-wide seam allowance on all sides. Measure the triangle from tip to base and add an extra ⅛" to determine the strip width.

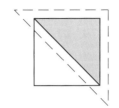

Finished-size bias square with ⅛"-wide seam allowance.

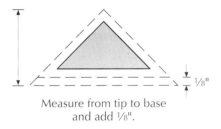

⅛"

Measure from tip to base and add ⅛".

MAKING QUARTER-SQUARE TRIANGLE UNITS

1. Cut 2 squares, 1 each from 2 contrasting fabrics, ¾" larger than the finished measurement of the quarter-square triangle unit. For miniatures, this measurement makes the finished unit slightly larger than needed to allow for squaring-up of the final unit for accuracy. For example, for a ¾" finished unit, cut the squares 1½". Each pair of squares yields 2 quarter-square triangle units.
2. On the wrong side of the lighter fabric, draw lines from corner to corner in both directions; it will look like an X. Draw a sewing line ⅛" from each side of one diagonal line.

3. Place the 2 squares right sides together. Stitch on the sewing lines.

4. Cut on the line between the rows of stitching; you will have 2 bias squares. Press the seam allowance toward the darker fabric. On the wrong side of 1 bias square, extend the drawn line onto the darker triangle so that it reaches from corner to corner. Draw a sewing line ⅛" from each side of this line.

5. Place the 2 bias squares right sides together; align the opposing seams and butt the seam allowances. Stitch on the sewing lines. Cut on the line between the rows of stitching. Open and press.

6. Square the resulting quarter-square triangle units to the correct size. Remember to trim all 4 sides of the unit, keeping the X in the center.

Trim.

MAKING STRIP-PIECED UNITS

Cut background pieces from strips, or combine strips to make four-patch and nine-patch units, checkerboards, and other combinations.

To cut strips:

1. Fold the fabric in half crosswise. Align the edge of a 4" square ruler with the fold of the fabric, then align a longer ruler with the left edge of the square; trim the raw edge. Align the required strip measurement on the long ruler with the cut edge of the fabric, and cut strips as required for your design.

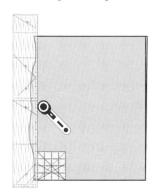

2. Crosscut squares and rectangles as required.

To make strip-pieced units:

1. Using a ⅛"-wide seam allowance, sew strips together in the order required for your design. If necessary, stabilize with Stitch-n-Tear. Press the seam allowances toward the darker fabric. Cut segments from the strip set as required for your design.

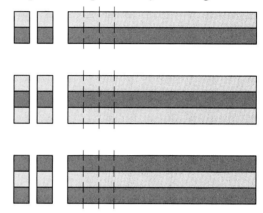

2. Stitch the segments together to form larger units or blocks.

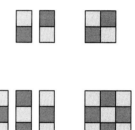

Appliquéing with Freezer Paper

There are many appliqué methods; everybody has a favorite. I have found that needleturn appliqué with freezer paper templates works best for miniature quilts. If you have a favorite method that works for you, use it.

NOTE: *Match the thread to the appliqué, not to the background fabric. Lightweight, 100% cotton machine-embroidery threads work well for appliqué, but are not available in a wide variety of colors. It is more important to match colors than to use a lightweight thread.*

1. Trace the appliqué pattern onto the dull (uncoated) side of freezer paper. Do not add seam allowances; cut the freezer-paper pieces the finished size of your pattern.

Freezer paper

Tip

Cut more than one freezer-paper template at a time. Trace a row of templates onto the dull side of the freezer paper. Layer 4 to 5 pieces of freezer paper and staple through the center of each traced template; cut through all layers. Leave the staple in place until you are ready to press the templates onto the fabric.

2. Preheat an iron to the wool setting. On a hard surface, press the freezer-paper pieces onto the *right side* of the fabric, shiny side down. Hold the iron to the count of 10.

3. Cut out the pieces, adding a ³⁄₁₆"-wide seam allowance. (A seam allowance of ¼" is too much and ⅛" is too little.)

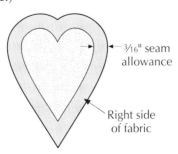

³⁄₁₆" seam allowance

Right side of fabric

4. To appliqué the pieces in place, with the tip of the needle, turn under the seam allowance up to the edge of the freezer paper, leaving a few threads showing. Blindstitch the appliqué in place (see below). If the curves are not smooth, trim the seam allowance a little.

5. Remove the paper when the appliqué is complete.

To do a blind stitch, choose thread that matches the color of the appliqué fabric, not the background fabric. Use a needle flexible enough to bend as you appliqué (page 6).

1. Knot the thread and bring the needle up from the wrong side of the background fabric. Catch 1 or 2 threads of the appliqué piece, and then bring the needle straight back down, as if you were falling off a cliff. (You don't slant as you fall off a cliff, you go straight down.) It doesn't matter if the needle hits the same hole or goes one thread in front or in back, as long as you go straight down.

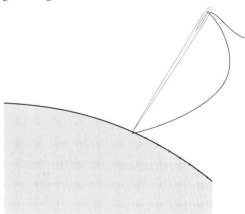

Bring the needle straight back down.

2. Bring the needle up ⅛" from the first stitch and repeat the process. Pull the thread tight enough that it blends into the appliqué, but not so tight that it distorts the shape.

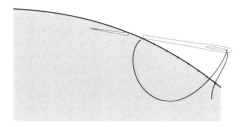

Appliquéing Tiny Stems

1. Cut strips (either bias or straight) 4 times the width of the finished stem. For example, for a ⅛"-wide stem, cut a ½"-wide strip. Press the strip in half lengthwise, wrong sides together.
2. Using a light table or a window, trace the stem placement from the appliqué diagram onto the background fabric.
3. Pin the folded strip in place, centering it over one of the drawn lines. Stitch the folded strips through the center, onto the background. This becomes one side of your stem. If the stem curves, stitch with the fold to the inside of the curve. When you fold the stem over, the finished edge is on the outside of the curve; this helps prevent puckers.

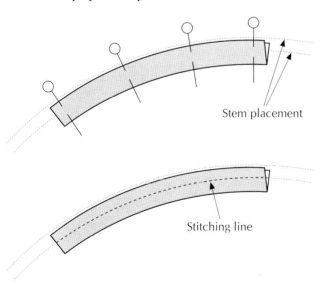

Stem placement

Stitching line

4. Trim the raw edge close to the stitching.

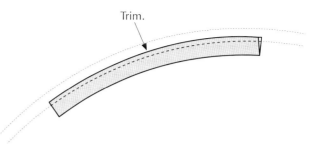

Trim.

5. Turn the folded edge over to cover the raw edge; blindstitch in place.

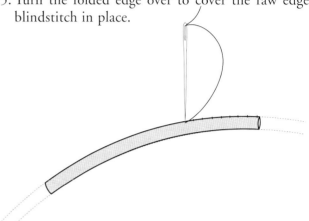

Pressing Seam Allowances

I jokingly tell my students, "Press it any way it will go." This advice applies in some cases, but here are a few guidelines.

- Press the seam allowances to one side or the other when possible. Press the seam allowances in opposite directions from row to row. Nest the seams to match them more easily.
- If necessary, press the seam allowances open to reduce bulk. Use your seam ripper to open the seam as you press and use an iron with a pointed tip.
- Press to preserve the continuity of the block, which does not necessarily mean toward the darker fabric. For example, with a House block, press the seam allowances toward the house so the windows and background recede and the house stands out. This makes the windows look like windows and the background look like the background. If you want a star to recede into the sky background, press the seam allowances toward the background.
- Use steam—it sets the seams more quickly.

GALLERY

Tulips-Go-Round

by Deborah L. White, 1991, Hansville, Washington, 14¼" x 14¼". Appliquéd Tulip blocks are surrounded by a meandering appliquéd tulip border. Instructions start on page 68.

Tall Timber

by Elaine Earl, 1996, Roy, Washington, 12¾" x 17¼". "Keep a green tree in your heart and perhaps the singing bird will come."—Chinese Proverb. This primitive tree pattern is a tribute to wonderful Washington, the Evergreen State. Design by Deborah L. White. Instructions start on page 49.

Bang for Your Buck
*by Deborah L. White, 1992, Hansville,
Washington, 12" x 14⅝". Bias squares
and four-patch units make up this
scrappy sampling of blocks.
Instructions start on page 35.*

Woven Through the Stars
*by Deborah Johnsen, 1996,
American Fork, Utah,
11¾" x 12¾". A scrappy star
variation of "Bang for Your Buck"
features the Ribbon Star block and
displays 200 different fabrics.*

Mini-Victory
by Joyce Becker, 1992,
Kent, Washington, 12½" x 12½".
Joyce re-created the traditional Jacob's
Ladder design with just one of the
"Bang for Your Buck" sampler blocks.

Jacob's Star
by Deborah Johnsen, 1996,
American Fork, Utah, 12¾" x 12¾".
Three hundred different fabrics combine
to create another scrappy wonder that
features the Stepping Stone block from the
"Bang for Your Buck" sampler.

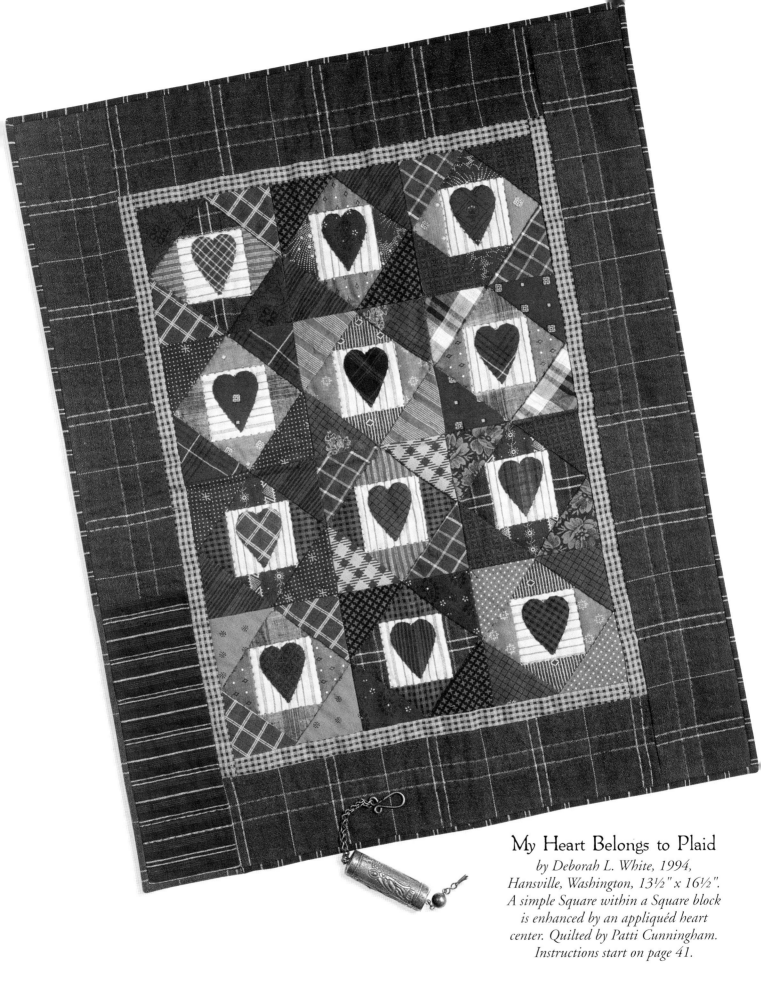

My Heart Belongs to Plaid

by Deborah L. White, 1994,
Hansville, Washington, 13½" x 16½".
A simple Square within a Square block
is enhanced by an appliquéd heart
center. Quilted by Patti Cunningham.
Instructions start on page 41.

An Angel to Watch Over Me

by Deborah L. White, 1994, Hansville, Washington, 10" x 13". "Be not forgetful to entertain strangers; for thereby some have entertained angels unawares."—Hebrews 13:2. A pictorial miniature quilt with a primitive country look, this charmer is loaded with miniature-quiltmaking techniques. Instructions start on page 52.

The Littlest Angel

by Mary Berdan, 1996, Bellevue, Washington, 5" x 6¼". A micro-mini version of "An Angel to Watch Over Me." Pattern on page 52.

Down-home Townhomes
by Deborah L. White, 1995,
Hansville, Washington, 10¾ x 19½".
Three primitive townhouses combine to
create this scrappy plaid neighborhood.
Quilted by Joyce Becker.
(Collection of Joyce Becker)
Instructions start on page 38.

Star Crazy:
Alberta's Constellation
by Mary Berdan, 1996,
Bellevue, Washington,
4¾" x 5¼".
Mary adapted the
¾" five-pointed star from
the top of "Down-home
Townhome #1" and used
it to create a micro-mini.
Design by
Deborah L. White.

Tumbler

by Deborah L. White, 1991,
Hansville, Washington, 9" x 11".
The charm of this traditional
one-template pattern lies in the
fabric selection and color placement.
Instructions start on page 32.

Spools

by Deborah L. White, 1990,
Hansville, Washington, 8¾" x 11¾".
An old-time favorite, the Spool block is
even more charming in miniature.
Instructions start on page 44.

Interlocking Ohio Stars

by Deborah L. White, 1995,
Hansville, Washington, 8½" x 10".
Two simple patches unite to create this impressive
interlocking star design. Quilted by Joyce Becker.
Instructions start on page 47.

On a Bender

by Deborah L. White, 1995, Hansville, Washington,
4¾" x 5¼". This is a micro-mini version of
"Interlocking Ohio Stars." I once received a phone call
from an editor at Miniature Quilts Magazine *informing*
me that one of my quilts had placed second in their
"Miniatures from the Heart" contest. My entry included
four ¾" Ohio Stars as part of the pattern. The editor
laughingly said that if I had included a couple more of
those little stars I probably would have received first place.
I thought about this from time to time over the next few
years and finally got up one morning, went on a bender,
and made an entire miniature quilt from ¾" Ohio Stars.

A Mini-Dresden Treat

*by Deborah L. White, 1995, Hansville, Washington,
14¼" x 17¼". Colorful mini-Dresden Plates are enhanced by
an inner border of Prairie Points. Instructions start on page 59.*

Yo-Yo's Garden

by Deborah L. White, 1996, Hansville,
Washington, 18" x 18". "Show me your garden,
and I shall tell you what you are."—Alfred Austin.
The Snowball blocks are enhanced by tiny
Yo-yo flowers. The Ice-Cream Cone
border adds charm to the design.
Instructions start on page 70.

Morning Glory

*by Mary Berdan, 1996, Bellevue,
Washington, 16½" x 16½".
A simple four-pointed star and
appliquéd petals create the Morning Glory
design. A scalloped border adds a
delightful finishing touch.
Design by Deborah L. White.
Instructions start on page 56.*

Fan-Itsies

by Deborah L. White, 1996,
Hansville, Washington,
16½" x 17". A diamond border
enhances embellished Fan blocks.
The three-dimensional appliquéd
border makes the final statement.
Instructions start on page 62.

Blackjack
by Deborah L. White, 1996,
Hansville, Washington,
15" x 15". Take a gamble with
this one. The unusual star blocks
are set with a pieced border
reminiscent of a game board.
Instructions start on page 74.

Tumbler

QUILT SIZE: 9" x 11"
BLOCK SIZE: 1"
SKILL LEVEL: BEGINNER
COLOR PHOTO: PAGE 25
TECHNIQUES:
Making an Accurate Template
Sewing with ⅛"-Wide Seam Allowances

Materials: 44"-wide fabric

¼ yd. *total* assorted scraps of light,
medium, and dark prints
for Tumbler blocks

⅛ yd. black stripe for
inner border and binding

⅛ yd. brown print for outer border

10" x 12" piece for backing

10" x 12" piece of batting

Cutting

See "Template Construction" on page 33.

From the light prints, cut:
16 tumbler pieces
From the medium prints, cut:
17 tumbler pieces
From the dark prints, cut:
16 tumbler pieces
From the black stripe, cut:
1 strip, ⅝" x 35", for the inner border
From the brown print, cut:
1 strip, 1¾" x 40", for the outer border

Template Construction

1. Place template material over the tumbler pattern on page 34. To trace the finished-size template (without the seam allowance) onto the template material, dot the seam intersections on the template, then use a ruler and an ultra-fine permanent marker to connect the dots. Double check the lines for accuracy.

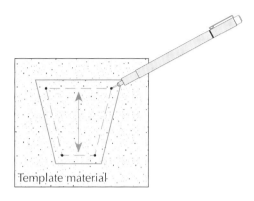

2. Place the template plastic on your cutting mat. Align the ⅛" mark of the ruler on the drawn line. Using a rotary cutter, cut out the template, adding a ⅛"-wide seam allowance on each side. Place the template on top of the original pattern to check for accuracy.

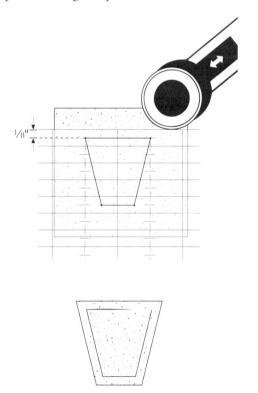

Assembly and Finishing

All seam allowances are ⅛" wide. Refer to "Basic Techniques" on pages 10–17 for construction methods. When stitching, be sure to use a piece of Stitch-n-Tear to stabilize the seams.

1. Arrange the tumbler pieces in 7 rows of 7 each. The first row is shown.

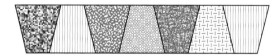

2. Start the second row with a tumbler placed wide side down. Arrange the fabrics so the same colors are not next to each other.
3. Check value placement. Arrange the pieces so your eyes travel throughout the quilt rather than staying in one spot.
4. When you are satisfied with the fabric placement, sew the tumblers together in rows, then join the rows. Press the seams in opposite directions from row to row, then join the rows.
5. Trim the 2 uneven edges so they are straight.

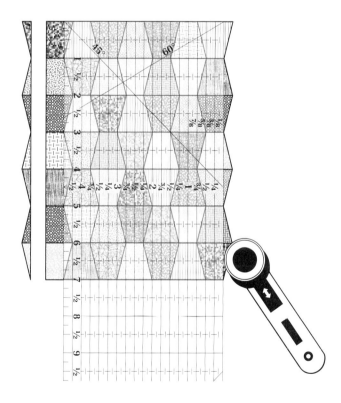

6. Referring to "Borders with Straight-Cut Corners" on page 77, measure the quilt top. From the ⅝"-wide inner-border strip, cut 2 borders to fit the top and bottom edges; stitch them to the quilt top. Add side borders in the same manner.

7. Using the 1¾"-wide brown strip, add outer borders.

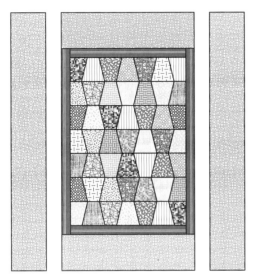

8. Layer the quilt top with batting and backing; baste.
9. Quilt as desired, or follow the quilting suggestion.

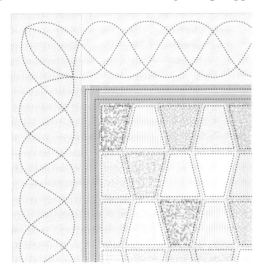

Quilting Suggestion

10. Bind the edges of the quilt. Referring to "Labeling Your Quilt" on page 81, add a label.

Potential Problems
and How to Solve Them

"The template is too big."

It is human nature to cut toward the outside of lines, which can make the template inaccurate. Adding the seam allowance to the template with the rotary cutter helps eliminate this problem.

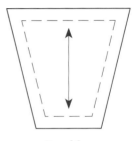

Tumbler
Template

Bang for Your Buck

QUILT SIZE: 12" x 14⅝"
BLOCK SIZE: 2¼"
SKILL LEVEL: BEGINNER
COLOR PHOTO: PAGE 20
TECHNIQUES:
Making Bias Squares
Strip-Piecing Four-Patch Units
Squaring Up

Materials: 44"-wide fabric

¼ yd. tan print for background
and sashing strips

⅛ yd. *total* assorted dark blue
fabrics for blocks. Choose
checks, stripes, and plaids.

⅛ yd. *total* assorted black fabrics for
blocks. Choose stripes and plaids.

⅛ yd. dark red plaid for blocks

⅛ yd. *total* assorted medium
red fabrics for blocks.
Choose checks and plaids.

⅛ yd. mustard plaid for blocks

⅛ yd. dark red print for blocks,
inner border, and binding

⅛ yd. black plaid #2 for
outer border

13" x 16" piece for backing

13" x 16" piece of batting

Cutting

From the tan print, cut:
1 strip, ⅝" x 39", for the four-patch units
1 strip, 1" x 26"; crosscut 24 squares, each 1" x 1",
for the background squares
8 strips, each ⅝" x 2½", for the sashing
3 strips, each ⅝" x 7¾", for the sashing
9 bias strips, each ¹⁵⁄₁₆" wide
From the assorted dark blue fabrics, cut:
3 bias strips, each ¹⁵⁄₁₆" wide
From the assorted black fabrics, cut:
3 bias strips, each ¹⁵⁄₁₆" wide
From the dark red plaid, cut:
3 bias strips, each ¹⁵⁄₁₆" wide
2 squares, each 1" x 1", for the Shoo Fly
and Single Irish Chain blocks
From the assorted red fabrics, cut:
2 strips, each ⅝" x 6", for the four-patch units
From the mustard plaid, cut:
1 strip, ⅝" x 27", for the four-patch units
1 square, 1" x 1", for the Windmill Blades block
From the dark red print, cut:
1 strip, ⅝" x 42", for the inner border
From the black plaid, cut:
2 strips, each 2" x 42", for the outer border

Construction

All seam allowances are ⅛" wide. Refer to "Basic Techniques" on pages 10–17 for construction methods. When stitching, be sure to use a piece of Stitch-n-Tear to stabilize the seams.

1. Pair each dark bias strip with a tan bias strip and sew them together along both long edges.

2. Referring to "Making Bias Squares" on pages 13–14, cut 49 assorted bias squares, each 1" x 1", from the pieced strips. The quilt in the photograph required 17 assorted red, 20 assorted blue, and 12 assorted black bias squares.

Make 49.

3. Sew the ⅝" x 39" tan strip and assorted dark strips together along 1 long edge. Press the seam toward the darker fabric.

4. From 1 unit, cut 4 segments, each 1" long, for the Churn Dash block.

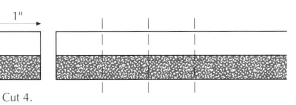

Cut 4.

5. From the remaining strips, cut ⅝"-wide segments. Sew them together in pairs to make four-patch units. Square up the four-patch units to 1".

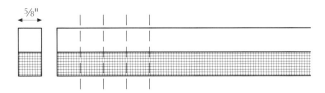

Make 28.

6. Referring to the block diagrams, arrange the assorted bias squares, four-patch units, and plain squares into blocks. Experiment with various color combinations. Use one block or many different blocks to create your quilt design.

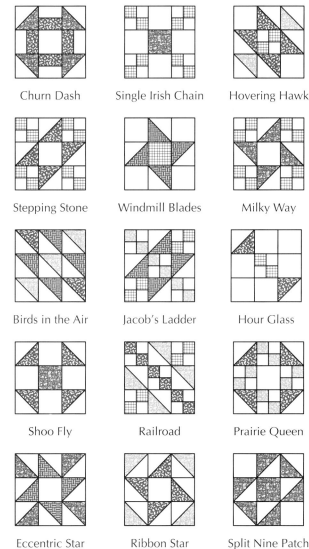

Churn Dash   Single Irish Chain   Hovering Hawk

Stepping Stone   Windmill Blades   Milky Way

Birds in the Air   Jacob's Ladder   Hour Glass

Shoo Fly   Railroad   Prairie Queen

Eccentric Star   Ribbon Star   Split Nine Patch

7. Sew the units together in rows. Press the seams in opposite directions from row to row, then join the rows.

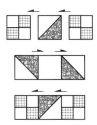

Assembly and Finishing

1. Arrange the blocks and ⅝" x 2½" sashing strips as shown below. Sew them together in rows. Press the seams toward the sashing strips.

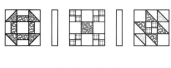

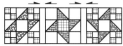

2. Arrange the rows and ⅝" x 7¾" sashing strips as shown and sew them together. Press the seams toward the sashing strips.

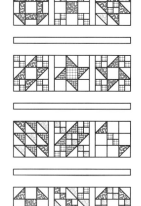

3. Referring to "Borders with Straight-Cut Corners" on page 77, measure the quilt top. From the ⅝"-wide inner border strip, cut 2 borders to fit the top and bottom edges and stitch them to the quilt top. Add side borders in the same manner.

4. Using the 2"-wide black plaid #2 strips, add the outer borders.

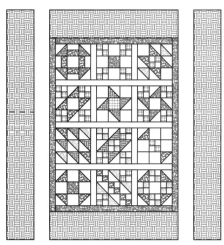

5. Layer the quilt top with batting and backing; baste.

6. Quilt as desired, or follow the quilting suggestion.

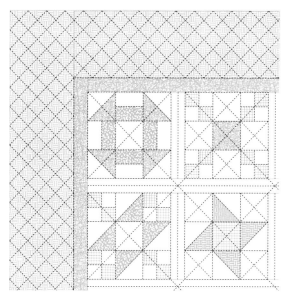

Quilting Suggestion

7. Bind the edges of the quilt with the dark red print. Referring to "Labeling Your Quilt" on page 81, add a label.

Potential Problems and How to Solve Them

"The bias strips become distorted."

Be sure to use Stitch-n-Tear as a stabilizer. Do not pull the strips as they feed through the sewing machine, just guide them. On some machines you can manually loosen or tighten the feed-dog pressure, look for this feature on the top left of the machine. Loosen the pressure slightly.

"The pieces don't fit together."

Square up both the four-patch units and the bias squares to the appropriate measurements. Make sure you use an accurate ⅛"-wide seam allowance, especially with the four-patch units.

Down-Home Townhomes

QUILT SIZE: 10¾" x 19½"

BLOCK SIZE: 1¼" x 2¾"

SKILL LEVEL:
BEGINNER/INTERMEDIATE

COLOR PHOTO: PAGE 24

TECHNIQUES:
Piecing with Paper Foundations
Piecing with Freezer-Paper Templates

Materials: 44"-wide fabric

⅛ yd. light print for
background and border #1

¼ yd. red plaid for
borders #2 and #4

⅛ yd. black print for
border #3 and binding

¼ yd. *total* assorted scraps of
medium and dark prints and plaids
for the houses

⅛ yd. light stripe for windows

20 pieces *total*, each 1½" x 2",
of assorted dark prints
and plaids for the roofs

4 pieces *total*, each 1¼" x 2",
of assorted mustard and
red scraps for the stars

12" x 21" piece for backing

12" x 21" piece of batting

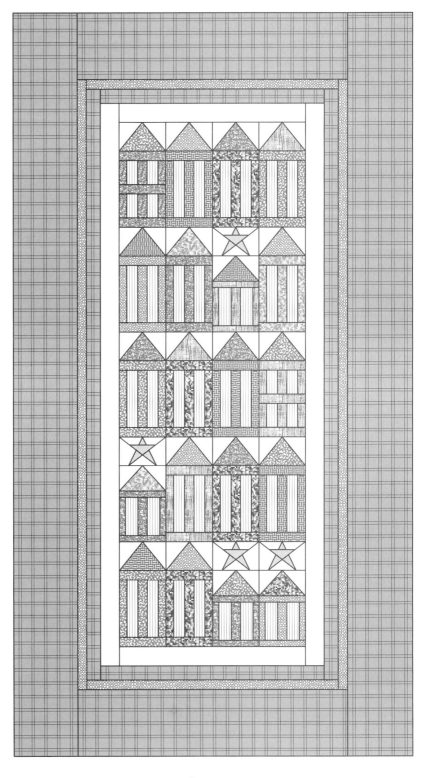

Cutting

From the light print, cut:
2 strips, each ¾" x 42", for border #1

From the red plaid, cut:
2 strips, each ⅝" x 42", for border #2
2 strips, each 2" x 42", for border #4

From the black print, cut:
2 strips, each ½" x 42", for border #3

Construction

All seam allowances are ⅛" wide. Refer to "Basic Techniques" on pages 10–17 for construction methods. When stitching, be sure to use a piece of Stitch-n-Tear to stabilize the seams. Use the templates and foundations on page 40.

1. Trace 4 House #1, 14 House #2, and 2 top sections and 2 bottom sections of House #3.
2. Referring to "Piecing with Paper Foundations" on page 12, construct 20 houses. Refer to the illustration to determine which pieces are background and which are house or window.

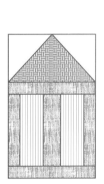 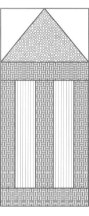 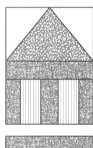

House #1   House #2   House #3

3. Join the top and bottom sections of House #3.

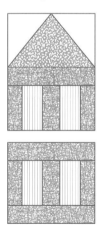 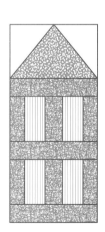

House #3

4. Trace 4 stars onto the dull (uncoated) side of freezer paper; label the pieces. Referring to "Piecing with Freezer-Paper Templates" on pages 11–12 and the piecing diagram below, cut out and assemble 4 stars. This is a good place to use gluestick on the seams (page 6), as the pieces are too small for pins.

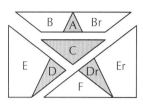

NOTE: *If you prefer, you can foundation paper-piece the stars in 3 sections using the foundations on page 40.*

5. Sew a star to the top of each House #1.

Assembly and Finishing

1. Referring to the quilt plan on page 38, arrange the houses in 5 rows of 4 houses each. Sew the houses together in rows, then sew the rows together.
2. Referring to "Borders with Straight-Cut Corners" on page 77, measure the quilt top. From the ⅝"-wide light print strip, cut 2 borders to fit the top and bottom edges and stitch them to the quilt top. Measure, cut, and add the side borders to the quilt top.
3. Add the 3 remaining borders in the same manner.

4. Layer the quilt top with batting and backing; baste.
5. Quilt as desired, or follow the quilting suggestion.

Quilting Suggestion

6. Bind the edges of the quilt. Referring to "Labeling Your Quilt" on page 81, add a label.

Potential Problems and How to Solve Them

"The star pieces were so small I lost them."

Put these babies in a safe place. Keep a small container next to your sewing machine to protect the star pieces from slight breezes. A flannel board (page 6) is also a good keeper and design surface.

"The star points aren't where they're supposed to be."

There are two solutions to this problem: Call it a free-form star and give it a name that will make you a true artist, or use a pin to line up the seams. Stick a pin through one seam and into the seam it is supposed to line up with. Apply a small amount of gluestick to the seam allowance only, and then stick the two pieces together. The glue should keep them from shifting.

CREATIVE OPTION

Try making a micro-mini quilt with just the Star block. Trim the block pattern as shown. See "Star Crazy: Alberta's Constellation" on page 24.

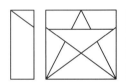

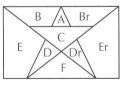

Full-Size Star Block

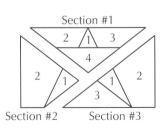

Foundation Option

Down-Home Townhomes
Foundations

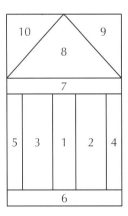

House #1

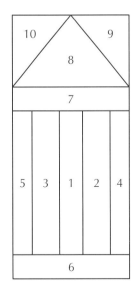

House #2

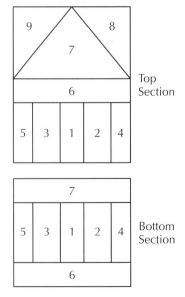

House #3

My Heart Belongs to Plaid

QUILT SIZE: 13½" x 16½"
BLOCK SIZE: 3"
SKILL LEVEL: BEGINNER
COLOR PHOTO: PAGE 22
TECHNIQUES:
Piecing with Paper Foundations
Appliquéing with Freezer Paper

Materials: 44"-wide fabric

⅛ yd. light print for center squares
⅛ yd. tan check for inner border
⅛ yd. blue plaid for outer border
⅜ yd. *total* assorted blue, brown,
    and red prints for blocks
2" x 7" scrap of blue plaid
    #2 for border
⅛ yd. black plaid #1 for binding
15" x 18" piece for backing
15" x 18" piece of batting

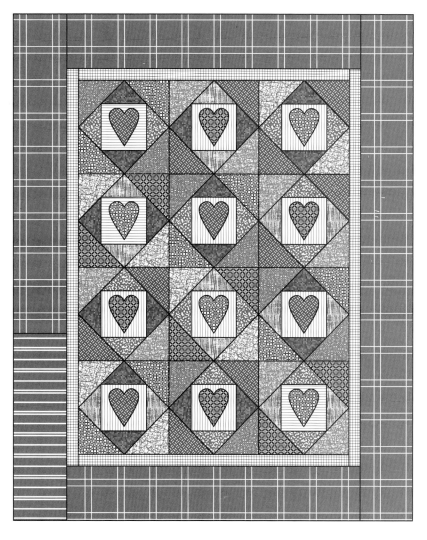

Cutting

From the light print, cut:
1 strip, 2" x 24"; crosscut 12 squares,
each 2" x 2", for the center squares
From the tan check, cut:
2 strips, each ⅝" x 42", for the inner border
From the blue plaid, cut:
2 strips, each 2" x 42", for the outer border
From a blue plaid scrap, cut:
1 rectangle, 2" x 7", for the outer border

Construction

All seam allowances are ⅛" wide. Refer to "Basic Techniques" on pages 10–17 for construction methods. When stitching, be sure to use a piece of Stitch-n-Tear to stabilize the seams.

1. Using the pattern on page 43, trace 12 Square within a Square blocks onto tracing paper. Referring to "Piecing with Paper Foundations" on pages 12–13, construct 12 blocks.

Make 12.

NOTE: *When cutting fabric for paper foundation piecing, do not try to cut an exact size. Cut chunks or strips that are at least ½" too large on all sides; then trim as you go.*

2. Arrange the blocks as shown. Sew them together in rows. Remove the freezer paper from the blocks when each row is complete. Sew the rows together.

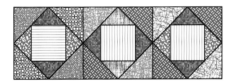

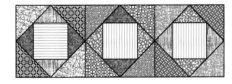

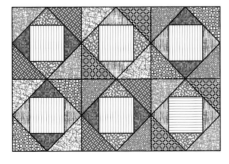

3. Using the template on page 43, cut 12 hearts from the assorted red prints. Referring to "Appliquéing with Freezer Paper" on pages 16–17, appliqué the hearts in place. Refer to the quilt plan on page 41 for placement.

Assembly and Finishing

1. Referring to "Borders with Straight-Cut Corners" on page 77, measure the quilt top. From the tan check strips, cut 2 borders to fit the top and bottom edges and sew them to the quilt top. Measure the quilt top again, and then cut the side borders and add them to the quilt top.

2. From the blue plaid #1 strips, cut 2 borders to fit the top and bottom edges and sew them to the quilt top. Sew the 2" x 7" rectangle of blue plaid #2 to the remaining strip of blue plaid #1, and then cut 2 borders to fit the side edges as shown. Add them to the quilt top.

3. Layer the quilt top with batting and backing; baste.
4. Quilt as desired, or follow the quilting suggestion.

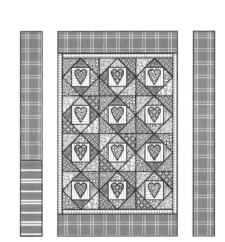

Quilting Suggestion

5. Bind the edges of the quilt. Referring to "Labeling Your Quilt" on page 81, add a label.

Potential Problems
and How to Solve Them

"When I piece on the foundation, the seam allowance aren't wide enough."

Be sure to cut your fabric pieces larger than you think you need; don't try to cut exact shapes. Remember to leave ⅛"-wide seam allowances around the outside edges of the foundation when you trim.

"The point of the heart is blunt."

To pull out the point and stabilize it, take 2 long stitches at the point before you turn.

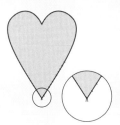

"The V of the heart is fraying."

Don't clip the V until you are ready to stitch; then take 2 stitches at the critical point and dot a little FrayCheck on the V. (Make sure to test the FrayCheck first; it may darken your fabric where applied.)

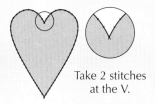

Take 2 stitches
at the V.

"The curve of the heart isn't smooth."

Trim your seam allowance a little more.

"The appliqué stitches show."

There are three possible reasons: the thread doesn't match, you may be slanting your stitches, or you may not be pulling your stitches tight enough.

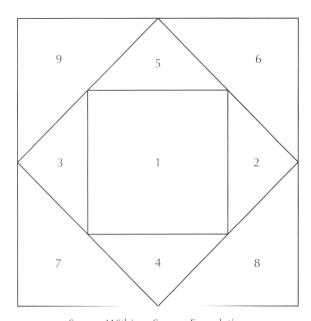

Square Within a Square Foundation

My Heart Belongs to Plaid
Template and Foundation

Heart Template

Spools

QUILT SIZE: 8¾" x 11¾"
BLOCK SIZE: 1½"
SKILL LEVEL: BEGINNER TO
INTERMEDIATE
COLOR PHOTO: PAGE 25
TECHNIQUES:
Setting In Seams
Piecing with Freezer-Paper Templates

Materials: 44"-wide fabric

¼ yd. *total* assorted scraps of medium
to dark prints for spools

¼ yd. *total* assorted scraps of light to
medium prints for background

⅛ yd. blue plaid for outer border

¾"-wide strips of assorted red prints
to total 30" for inner border

⅛ yd. tan plaid for binding

10" x 13" piece for backing

10" x 13" piece of batting

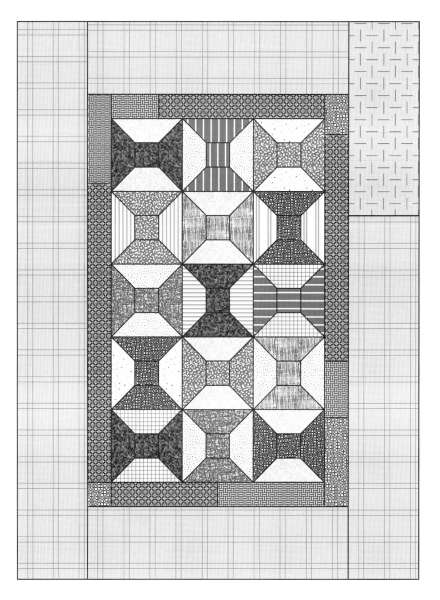

Cutting

Use the templates on page 46.
From the prints for spools, cut:
30 *total* Template A*
15 *total* Template B*
1 rectangle, 1¾" x 4½", for border
From the assorted light to medium prints, cut:
30 *total* Template A. Cut 2 from the same fabric for each spool.
From the blue plaid, cut:
1 strip, 1¾" x 36", for the outer border
Cut 2 Template A and 1 Template B from the same fabric for each spool.

Construction

All seam allowances are ⅛" wide. Refer to "Basic Techniques" on pages 10–17 for construction methods. When stitching, be sure to use a piece of Stitch-n-Tear to stabilize the seams.

1. Using the pattern on page 46, trace the full-size block diagram onto the dull (uncoated) side of freezer paper. Trace 15 blocks; label the pieces.
2. Carefully cut the pieces apart to make templates.
3. Spacing the templates to allow for ⅛"-wide seam allowances, press them, shiny side down, onto the wrong side of the appropriate fabrics.

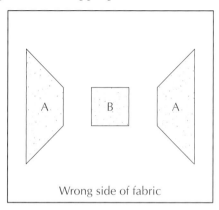

Wrong side of fabric

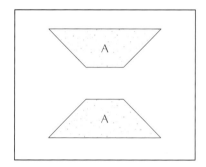

4. Cut out the pieces, using a rotary cutter and ruler and adding a ⅛"-wide seam allowance. Leave the freezer paper attached.

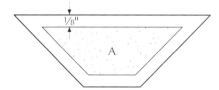

5. Referring to "Piecing with Freezer-Paper Templates" on pages 11–12 and to the piecing diagram below, join 2 piece A to each matching piece B. Start and stop the stitching at the corners of the freezer paper. Do not stitch into the seam allowance.

Begin and end stitching
at the corner of the freezer paper.

6. To set in background piece A, first sew piece A to square B. Begin and end the stitching at the corners of the freezer paper (the seam intersections). Next, join the A pieces; stitch from the inner to the outer corners as shown.

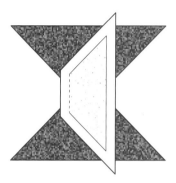

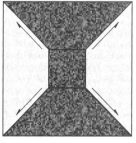

Make 15.

Assembly and Finishing

1. Arrange the blocks as shown in the quilt plan on page 44.
2. Sew the blocks together in rows; press the seams in opposite directions from row to row.
3. Sew the ¾"-wide red print strips together as shown to make 1 long strip.

30"

4. Referring to "Borders with Straight-Cut Corners" on page 77, measure the quilt top. From the pieced red strip, cut 2 strips to fit the top and bottom edges and sew them to the quilt top. Measure the quilt top again, then cut the side borders and add them to the quilt top.
5. From the blue plaid, cut 2 strips to fit the top and bottom edges; sew them to the quilt top. Sew the 1¾" x 4½" dark print rectangle to the remaining blue plaid strip. Then cut 2 strips to fit the side edges and add them to the quilt top as shown.

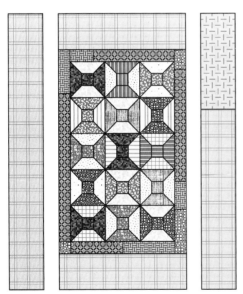

6. Layer the quilt top with batting and backing; baste.

7. Quilt as desired, or follow the quilting suggestion.

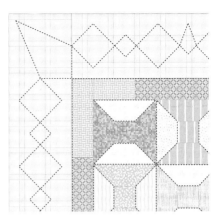

Quilting Suggestion

8. Bind the edges of the quilt. Referring to "Labeling Your Quilt" on page 81, add a label.

Potential Problems and How to Solve Them

"The pieces don't turn smoothly when I try to stitch the diagonal seams."

Be careful not to stitch into the seam allowance. If you sew into the seam allowance, nothing works right.

"The diagonal seams are stretching."

Leave the freezer paper on until after you have finished the entire block. The freezer paper stabilizes the bias edges.

"The spools don't lie flat."

Press the block and it should settle down. Make sure you used the edge of the freezer paper as your guide when stitching and that you did not stitch into the seam allowance.

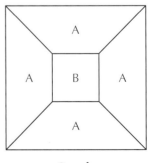

Spools
Templates

Interlocking Ohio Stars

QUILT SIZE: 8½" x 10"
BLOCK SIZE: ¾"
SKILL LEVEL: INTERMEDIATE
COLOR PHOTO: PAGE 26
TECHNIQUE:
Making Quarter-Square Triangle Units

Materials: 44"-wide fabric

⅛ yd. *total* assorted navy blue, black, and red prints for stars

⅛ yd. *total* assorted light prints for background

⅛ yd. navy blue stripe for inner border

⅛ yd. navy blue plaid #1 for outer border and binding

1½" x 3½" rectangle navy blue plaid #2 for border

10" x 12" piece for backing

10" x 12" piece of batting

Cutting

From the assorted prints for stars, cut:
16 squares, each 1½" x 1½", for the star points
12 squares, each 1" x 1", for the star centers
From the assorted light prints, cut:
16 squares, each 1½" x 1½"
20 squares, each 1" x 1"
From the navy blue stripe, cut:
1 strip, ½" x 28"
From the navy blue plaid #1, cut:
1 strip, 1½" x 32"

Construction

All seam allowances are ⅛" wide. Refer to "Basic Techniques" on pages 10–17 for construction methods. When stitching, be sure to use a piece of Stitch-n-Tear to stabilize the seams.

1. Referring to "Making Quarter-Square Triangle Units" on pages 14–15, layer a light print 1½" x 1½" square with a dark square. Mark and stitch. Repeat with the remaining 15 pairs of squares.
2. Measure the quarter-square triangle units and, if necessary, square them up so they measure 1" x 1".

Make 31.

Assembly and Finishing

1. Referring to the quilt plan on page 47, arrange the quarter-square triangle units and 1" light print and dark squares into 9 rows of 7 squares each.
2. Sew the blocks together into rows; press the seams in opposite directions from row to row.
3. Sew the rows together, placing a dab of gluestick at the seam allowances as you match them.
4. Referring to "Borders with Straight-Cut Corners" on page 77, measure the quilt top. From the navy blue stripe, cut 2 borders to fit the top and bottom edges and stitch them to the quilt top. Cut 2 borders to fit the side edges; sew them to the quilt top.
5. From the 1½"-wide strip of navy blue plaid, cut 2 borders to fit the top and bottom edges; sew them to the quilt top. Stitch the 1½" x 3½" navy blue plaid #2 rectangle to the remaining plaid #1 border strip. Cut 2 borders to fit the side edges; sew them to the quilt top.

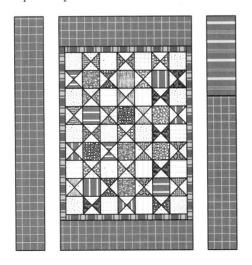

6. Layer the quilt top with batting and backing; baste.
7. Quilt as desired, or follow the quilting suggestion.

Quilting Suggestion

8. Bind the edges of the quilt with navy blue plaid #1. Referring to "Labeling Your Quilt" on page 81, add a label.

Potential Problems and How to Solve Them

"The quarter-square triangles are larger than the plain patches and the pieces don't fit together."

The quarter-square triangles are larger than needed. Make sure they are squared to the correct size.

CREATIVE OPTION

Try making a micro-mini quilt with ¼" finished (½" cut) quarter-square triangle units. Use 1" x 1" squares for the star points. The trick is to use a gluestick to keep the pieces together while you stitch. Also, be sure to use Stitch-n-Tear to stabilize the seams and a seam ripper to guide the fabric through the machine. See "On a Bender" on page 26.

Tall Timber

QUILT SIZE: 12¾" x 17¼"
BLOCK SIZE: 1½" x 3"
SKILL LEVEL: INTERMEDIATE
COLOR PHOTO: page 19
TECHNIQUES:
Piecing with Freezer Paper
Piecing with Paper Foundations
Constructing Strip-Pieced Units
Appliquéing with Freezer Paper

Materials: 44"-wide fabric

¼ yd. green plaid for
trees and border

¼ yd. light solid for background

⅛ yd. red print for tree accents,
middle border, and binding

¼ yd. green print for tree and leaves

⅛ yd. mustard print for trees

14"x 19" piece for backing

14" x 19" piece of batting

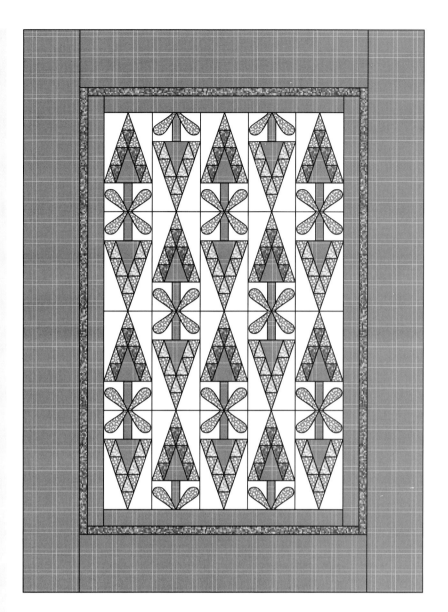

Cutting

From the green plaid, cut:
1 strip, ½" x 27", for the tree trunk
2 strips, each ¾" x 42", for the inner border
2 strips, each 2" x 42", for the outer border
From the light solid, cut:
2 strips, each ⅞" x 27", for the tree-trunk section
From the red print, cut:
2 strips, each ⅓" x 40", for the middle border

Construction

All seam allowances are ⅛" wide. Refer to "Basic Techniques" on pages 10–17 for construction methods. When stitching, be sure to use a piece of Stitch-n-Tear to stabilize the seams. Use the templates on page 51.

1. From freezer paper, cut 20 *each* of templates A, B, and B reversed.

2. Using a dry iron on the wool setting, press the freezer-paper templates, shiny side down, onto the wrong side of the appropriate fabrics (count to 10). Space the templates to allow for ⅛"-wide seam allowances. Using a rotary cutter and ruler, cut out the pieces, adding a ⅛"-wide seam allowance. Leave the freezer paper attached.

3. Using a ⅛"-wide seam allowance, stitch a ⅞"-wide light solid strip to each side of the ½"-wide green plaid strip. Crosscut the strip set at 1¼" intervals.

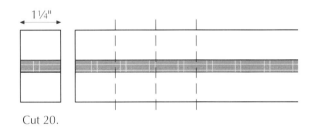

Cut 20.

4. Trace the tree sections on page 51 onto tracing paper with a black permanent marker. Number the foundations as indicated on each pattern. You will need 20 of each section.

5. Referring to "Piecing with Paper Foundations" on pages 12–13, construct the tree sections. Make 10 of each section with the green and mustard prints, and the remaining 10 of each section with the green and red prints.

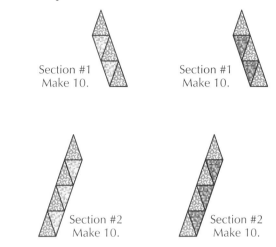

Section #1
Make 10.

Section #1
Make 10.

Section #2
Make 10.

Section #2
Make 10.

6. Stitch section 1 to the right side of piece A; then add section 2 to the left side.

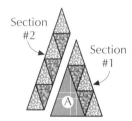

Section #2

Section #1

A

7. Sew pieces B and B reversed to the tree section. Add the trunk section.

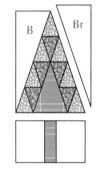

B   Br

Assembly and Finishing

1. Arrange the blocks as shown in the quilt plan on page 49; sew them together. Press seams in opposite directions from row to row.

2. Referring to "Appliquéing with Freezer Paper" on pages 16–17, appliqué the leaves to each trunk section. (Do not appliqué the leaves before stitching the blocks together; it would create too much bulk.) Refer to the quilt plan for placement.

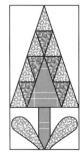

3. Referring to "Borders with Straight-Cut Corners" on page 77, measure the quilt top. From the ¾"-wide green plaid strip, cut 2 pieces to fit the top and bottom edges; sew them to the quilt top. Cut 2 pieces to fit the side edges; sew them to the quilt top.

4. Add the ½"-wide red middle border in the same manner, then add the 2"-wide green plaid outer border.

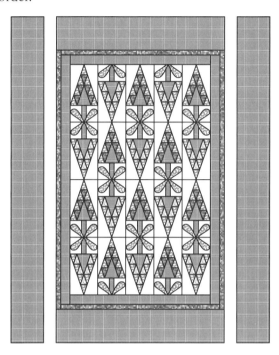

5. Layer the quilt top with batting and backing; baste.
6. Quilt as desired, or follow the quilting suggestion.

Quilting Suggestion

7. Bind the edges of the quilt. Referring to "Labeling Your Quilt" on page 81, add a label.

Potential Problems and How to Solve Them

"The tree sections don't match up."

Pin the inside seam first; then match the outer edges.

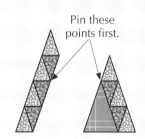

Pin these points first.

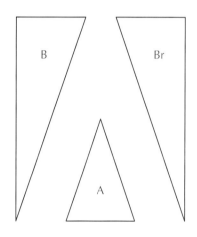

B   Br

A

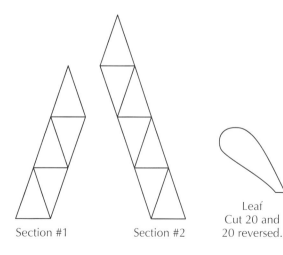

Section #1   Section #2

Leaf
Cut 20 and
20 reversed.

Tall Timber
Templates and Foundations

An Angel to Watch Over Me

QUILT SIZE: 10" x 13"
SKILL LEVEL: INTERMEDIATE
COLOR PHOTO: PAGE 23
TECHNIQUES:
Making Bias Squares
Strip-Piecing Checkerboards
Piecing with Freezer-Paper Templates
Piecing with Paper Foundations
Appliquéing with Freezer Paper

Materials: 44"-wide fabric

¼ yd. light print for background

⅜ yd. *total* assorted dark and
light scraps of blue, red, green,
gold, brown, tan, and black
prints and plaids

⅛ yd. blue print for
middle border

¼ yd. blue plaid for
outer border

12" x 15" piece for backing

12" x 15" piece of batting

⅛ yd. brown plaid for binding

Embroidery floss in a variety
of colors for flowers
and angel's halo

Cutting

From the light print, cut:

1 rectangle, 3¼" x 4¼", for the Angel block
1 rectangle, 1¼" x 3¼", for the Moon block
1 rectangle, 1¼" x 1¾", for the Moon block
2 bias strips, each ¹³⁄₁₆" x 12", for the Star blocks
and border bias squares
8 squares, each ¾" x ¾", for the Star blocks
1 strip, ¾" x 32", for the inner border

From the assorted scraps, cut:

1 light strip, ¾" x 12", for the checkerboard
1 dark strip, ¾" x 12", for the checkerboard
2 bias strips, each ¹³⁄₁₆" x 12",
for the Star blocks and border bias squares
2 squares, each ¾" x ¾", for the Star block centers

Continued on next page.

From the blue print, cut:
1 strip, ¾" x 34", for the middle border
From the blue plaid, cut:
2 strips, each 1¾" x 42", for the outer border

Construction

All seam allowances are ⅛" wide. Refer to "Basic Techniques" on pages 10–17 for construction methods. When stitching, be sure to use a piece of Stitch-n-Tear to stabilize the seams.

1. Using the pattern on page 82, trace 1 House block onto the dull (uncoated) side of freezer paper. Label the pieces and cut them out. Iron them, shiny side down, to the wrong sides of the assorted scraps.

2. Referring to "Piecing with Freezer-Paper Templates" on pages 11–12, construct 1 House block.

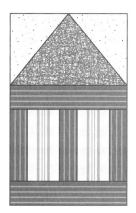

House Block

3. Using the foundations on page 82, trace Tree blocks #1 and #2 onto tracing paper. Do not add seam allowances. Number the pieces as shown. Referring to "Piecing with Paper Foundations" on pages 12–13, construct each Tree block. Use the same dark fabric for piece #4 of Tree #1 that you will use for the checkerboard section.

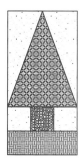 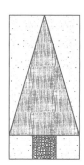

Tree #1   Tree #2

4. Place the dark and light ¾" x 12" strips right sides together, and sew them together along one long edge. Press the seam toward the dark fabric. Crosscut the strip set at ¾" intervals for a total of 8 segments.

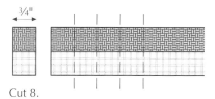

Cut 8.

5. Sew the segments together to make one 3-piece section and one 5-piece section. Stitch the 3-piece section to the bottom of Tree block #2 and add the 5-piece section to the bottom of the House block.

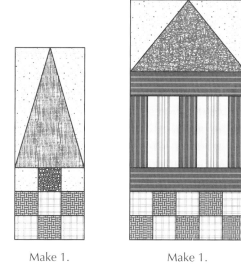

Make 1.   Make 1.

6. Place 1 dark and 1 light ¹³⁄₁₆" x 12" bias strip right sides together; stitch along both long edges. Referring to "Making Bias Squares" on pages 13–14, cut ¾" x ¾" bias-square units from the pieced strip. Press the seams toward the dark fabric, then square up the units. Repeat with the remaining bias strips. Make a total of 23 bias squares.

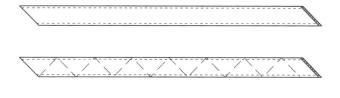

Make 23.

7. Arrange four bias squares with four ¾" light print squares and one dark square as shown; sew the squares together to complete a Star block. Make 2 Star blocks.

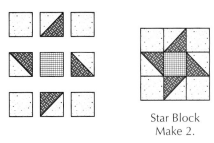

Star Block
Make 2.

Assembly and Finishing

1. Arrange the units and sew them together as shown to complete the quilt top.

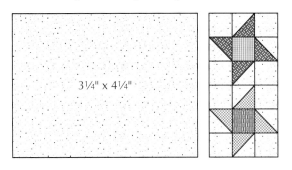

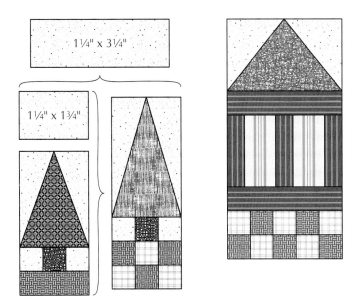

2. Referring to "Borders with Straight-Cut Corners" on page 77, measure the quilt top. Cut 2 borders from the ¾" x 32" light print strip to fit the top and bottom edges. Sew them to the quilt top. Measure the quilt top again, then cut 2 borders to fit the side edges and add them to the quilt top.

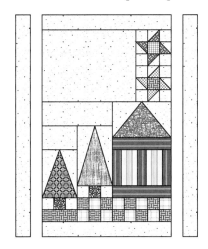

3. Trace the angel and moon templates on page 82 onto the dull (uncoated) side of freezer paper. Number the pieces and cut them out.

4. Referring to "Appliquéing with Freezer Paper" on pages 16–17, appliqué the angel and moon in position as shown on the quilt plan. Appliqué the pieces in numerical sequence. Embroider a halo around the angel's head.

5. Cut the blue ¾" x 34" border strip into several pieces and add bias squares at random, referring to the quilt plan on page 52. From the pieced strip, cut 2 borders to fit the top and bottom edges; sew them to the quilt top. Measure the quilt top, then cut and add the side borders.

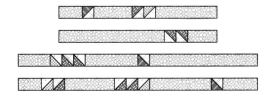

6. Using the 1¾"-wide blue plaid strips, add the outer borders in the same manner.

7. Layer the quilt top with batting and backing; baste.

8. Quilt as desired, or follow the quilting suggestion.

Quilting Suggestion

9. Embroider flowers on the Tree and House blocks if desired. Refer to the photo on page 23.

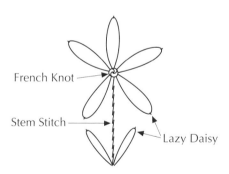

French Knot

Stem Stitch

Lazy Daisy

Straight Stitch

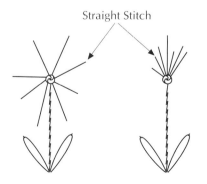

10. Bind the edges of the quilt. Referring to "Labeling Your Quilt" on page 81, add a label.

CREATIVE OPTION

Use the actual-size quilt plan on page 52 to make a micro-mini quilt: "The Littlest Angel" (page 23). Trace the appropriate pieces for paper foundations, freezer-paper piecing, and appliqué. The bias squares in this tiny charmer are ¼" finished, and the strips for the checkerboard are cut ½" wide.

Potential Problems and How to Solve Them

"The checkerboard sections don't fit the House and Tree blocks."

First, press the seams open. This is one of those quilting rules that can be broken when it comes to miniature quilts. Second, modify your seam allowance to a scant ⅛" wide. Unfortunately, you won't know you have the problem until after you have sewn the pieces together, so you may have to redo the seams. Finally, always make sure your seam allowance is accurate, especially where you have multiple seams.

"The stars aren't going together smoothly."

Take time to square up your bias squares. An extra minute saves you many frustrating moments later on.

"The curves on the appliqué are not turning under smoothly."

The seam allowance is too wide; trim it a bit.

"The freezer paper on the appliqué falls off."

Use a very hot iron and press for the full 10 seconds. Press on a hard surface, such as a bread board. Do not pin the piece on until you are ready to appliqué because the pin will release the hold of the freezer paper on the fabric.

Morning Glory

QUILT SIZE: 16½" x 16½"
BLOCK SIZE: 2¾"
SKILL LEVEL: INTERMEDIATE
COLOR PHOTO: PAGE 29
TECHNIQUES:
Piecing with Paper Foundations
Appliquéing with Freezer Paper
Making a Scalloped Border

Materials: 44"-wide fabric

½ yd. light solid for background, borders, and binding

⅛ yd. yellow solid for star centers

⅛ yd. pink print for petals and middle border

⅛ yd. blue print for stars, corner squares, and border petals

18" x 18" piece for backing

18" x 18" piece of batting

Cutting

From the light solid, cut:
2 strips, each 1¼" x 42"; crosscut
64 squares, each 1¼" x 1¼", for the blocks
2 strips, each ¾" x 42", for the inner border
2 strips, each 3" x 42", for the outer border

From the yellow solid, cut:
1 strip, 1" x 18"; crosscut 16 segments, each 1" x 1", for the star centers

From the pink print, cut:
2 strips, each ½" x 42", for the middle border

From the blue print, cut:
4 squares, each ½" x ½", for the middle border

Construction

All seam allowances are ⅛" wide. Refer to "Basic Techniques" on pages 10–17 for construction methods. When stitching, be sure to use a piece of Stitch-n-Tear to stabilize the seams.

1. Using the pattern on page 83, trace 64 star-point foundations onto tracing paper. Number the pieces.
2. Referring to "Piecing with Paper Foundations" on pages 12–13, construct 64 star points from the remaining light solid and blue print fabrics.

Make 64.

3. Arrange 4 star points with 1 yellow square and 4 light solid squares; sew the pieces together as shown to complete a block. Make 16 blocks.

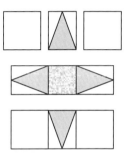 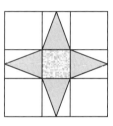

Make 16.

4. Arrange the blocks as shown in the quilt plan on page 56. Sew the blocks together in rows; sew the rows together.
5. Using the template on page 83, trace 64 petals onto freezer paper. Cut them out and press them, shiny side down, onto the right side of the remaining pink print. Cut the petals out and appliqué them in place on the light solid squares. Refer to "Appliquéing with Freezer Paper" on pages 16–17.

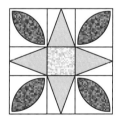

Assembly and Finishing

1. Referring to "Borders with Mitered Corners" on pages 78–79, measure the quilt top. From the ¾"-wide light solid strip, crosscut 4 strips to fit; sew them to the quilt top and miter the corners.
2. Referring to "Borders with Corner Squares" on pages 77–78, measure the quilt top, then cut 4 borders to fit from the ½"-wide pink print strip. Sew the blue print squares to each end of 2 pink strips. Add the short borders to the top and bottom edges of the quilt top; then add the long borders to the side edges as shown.

3. Add the 3"-wide light solid border, mitering the corners.
4. Trace and cut 12 petals from freezer paper. Iron them, shiny side down, onto the right side of the remaining blue print. Cut out the petals, adding ³⁄₁₆"-wide seam allowances, and appliqué them to the corners of the outer border. Refer to the quilt plan for placement.
5. Trace the scalloped border on page 83 onto the dull (uncoated) side of freezer paper, connecting the ends at the dashed lines. Cut out the border template.

6. Iron the freezer-paper template to the outer border, aligning the long straight edge with the edge of the middle border. Trace the scallop with a water-soluble pen. Repeat on the remaining 3 sides, reusing the same freezer-paper template.

Trace scallop onto outer border.

7. Layer the quilt top with batting and backing; baste.
8. Quilt as desired, or follow the quilting suggestion. Do not quilt within ⅛" of the marked scalloped edge.

Quilting Suggestion

9. From the binding fabric, cut 1⅛"-wide bias strips and join them to make the binding as shown on page 80. Pin the binding to the front of the quilt, following the marked scallop. Stitch the binding in place without stretching it, using a ⅛"-wide seam allowance. To stitch in the V of the scallop, spread the V into a straight line; clip the V if necessary. When you turn the binding and stitch it to the other side, it will form a miter.

10. Trim the excess border fabric even with the raw edge of the binding. Fold the binding to the back of the quilt and stitch in place. Referring to "Labeling Your Quilt" on page 81, add a label.

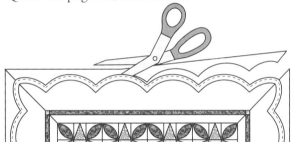

Cut away excess.

Potential Problems and How to Solve Them

"The scallops are cupped."

Gently ease the bias binding around the curves, being careful not to stretch it as you stitch.

A Mini Dresden Treat

QUILT SIZE: 14¼" x 17¼"
BLOCK SIZE: 2½"
SKILL LEVEL: INTERMEDIATE TO
ADVANCED
COLOR PHOTO: PAGE 27
TECHNIQUES:
Making Quick Dresden Plate Points
Appliquéing Circles
Making Prairie Points

Materials: 44"-wide fabric

½ yd. light solid for background
¼ yd. *total* assorted yellow prints
¼ yd. *total* assorted pink prints
¼ yd. *total* assorted blue prints
¼ yd. *total* assorted black prints
for blocks and binding
4" x 6" scrap of rose print for centers
16" x 19" piece for backing
16" x 19" piece of batting

Cutting

Use the templates on page 61.
From the light solid, cut:
1 rectangle, 10¼" x 14¼"
2 strips, each 1¾" x 42", for the outer border
From the assorted yellow prints, cut:
1 strip, 1¼" x 42", for the blocks
1 strip, 1" x 30", for the Prairie Points
From the assorted pink prints, cut:
1 strip, 1¼" x 42", for the blocks
1 strip, 1" x 30", for the Prairie Points
From the assorted blue prints, cut:
1 strip, 1¼" x 42", for the blocks
1 strip, 1" x 30", for the Prairie Points
From the assorted black prints, cut:
1 strip, 1¼" x 42", for the blocks
1 strip, 1" x 30", for the Prairie Points
From the rose print, cut:
12 Template C

Construction

All seam allowances are ⅛" wide. Refer to "Basic Techniques" on pages 10–17 for construction methods. When stitching, be sure to use a piece of Stitch-n-Tear to stabilize the seams.

1. Using the patterns on page 61, cut 1 Template A and 1 Template C from template material.

2. From each 1¼"-wide print strip, cut 36 Template A. Flip the template as shown to cut the pieces. Cut a total of 144 Template A.

Flip template and cut.

3. Fold each piece A lengthwise as shown, right sides together. Sew across the wide end, starting at the cut edge. Backstitch at the fold for extra strength. Turn the unit right side out and press the point.

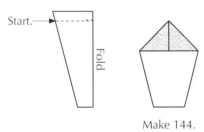

Make 144.

4. Sew the A pieces together in pairs, stitching from the wide end to the narrow end.

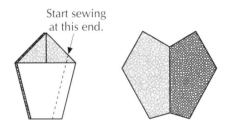

5. Stitch 3 pairs together. Make a second set of 3 pairs, and then join the 2 units to form a Dresden Plate. Press all seams in one direction.

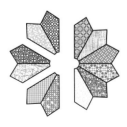

Make 12.

6. Fold the light solid rectangle as shown; lightly press to crease. Center a Dresden Plate in each creased square and appliqué in place.

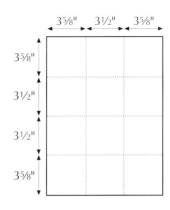

7. Cut 12 Template B from medium-weight paper. (The subscription cards in magazines are perfect.)

8. Sew a running stitch around the outside edge of each rose piece C. Place the paper circle on the wrong side of the fabric and pull the ends of the thread to gather the fabric around the paper. Press, and then remove the paper.

Pull thread to gather around paper circle.

9. Appliqué a circle in the center of each Dresden Plate, stitching through the background fabric to anchor the circle.

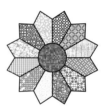

Appliqué circle in place.

Assembly and Finishing

1. Crosscut the 1"-wide print strips into 1" x 1" squares. Fold each square in half diagonally and press; then fold in half again and press to make Prairie Points.

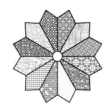

Make 86.

2. Place the first Prairie Point at the center of one side, raw edges even, and then add another at each end. Make sure the folded edges point in the same direction. Pin or glue the Prairie Points in position.

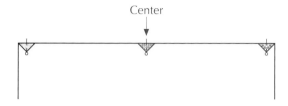

3. Placing each triangle inside another to make a continuous line, add Prairie Points until one side of the quilt is full. There are 24 Prairie Points on each side border and 19 on the top and bottom borders.

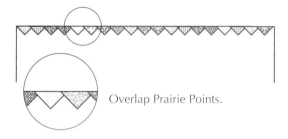

Overlap Prairie Points.

4. At the corners of the quilt top, fit 2 Prairie Points side by side as shown; they should not overlap. Baste in place.

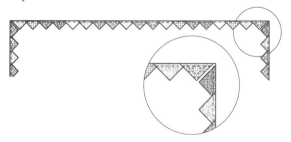

5. Referring to "Borders with Mitered Corners" on pages 78–79, measure the quilt top. From the 1¾"-wide light solid strips, cut 4 borders to fit; sew them to the quilt top, catching the Prairie Points in the seam. Miter the corners.

6. Layer the quilt top with batting and backing; baste.

7. Quilt as desired, or follow the quilting suggestion.

Quilting Suggestion

8. Bind the edges of the quilt with the remaining black print. Referring to "Labeling Your Quilt" on page 81, add a label.

Potential Problems and How to Solve Them

"The Prairie Points won't lie flat."

Tack each one down at the tip.

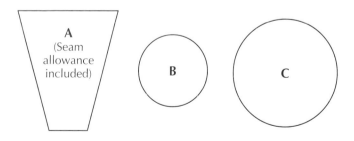

A Mini Dresden Treat
Templates

Fan-Itsies

QUILT SIZE: 16½" x 17"

BLOCK SIZE: 2½"

SKILL LEVEL: INTERMEDIATE TO ADVANCED

COLOR PHOTO: PAGE 30

TECHNIQUES:
Piecing with Paper Foundations
Using Seminole Piecing
Making Three-Dimensional Appliqués

Materials: 44"-wide fabric

½ yd. light solid for background, borders, and binding (If you are not making the appliqué border, select ¼ yd. of a coordinating floral print for the outer border.)

⅛ yd. *total* assorted dark, medium, and light blue prints

⅛ yd. *total* assorted dark, medium, and light rose prints

⅛ yd. *total* assorted dark, medium, and light purple prints

Optional: ¼ yd. green print for stems and leaves

Optional: 4" x 4" piece of dark yellow print for flower centers

18" x 19" piece for backing

18" x 19" piece of batting

1 package Sulky® Solvy™

Lace or doilies for embellishment

Assorted seed beads

Embroidery floss in lavender and black

Cutting

From the light solid, cut:

13 squares, each 2¾" x 2¾", for the Fan blocks

2 strips, each ⅞" x 42", for the diamond border; crosscut 2 strips, each ⅞" x 15", and 6 strips, each ⅞" x 9"

4 strips, each 2½" x 22", for the outer border

2 squares, each 5½" x 5½"; cut each square twice diagonally for 8 side setting triangles (The squares are larger than necessary to allow for trimming the quilt to size.)

2 squares, each 2¾" x 2¾"; cut each square once diagonally for 4 corner triangles

Continued on next page.

Use the templates on page 84.

From the dark blue print, cut:
1 strip, ⅝" x 15", for the diamond border
From the medium blue print, cut:
1 strip, ⅝" x 9", for the diamond border
From the assorted blue prints, cut:
4 Template D
10 Template F
24 squares, each 1" x 1", for the forget-me-nots
From the assorted rose prints, cut:
1 strip, ⅝" x 9", for the diamond border
8 Template C, for the appliqué border
2 Template D, for the appliqué border
20 Template F, for the appliqué border
12 Template G, for the appliqué border
From the purple prints, cut:
1 strip, ⅝" x 9", for the diamond border
8 Template C, for the appliqué border
From the light purple print, cut:
8 Template C, for the appliqué border
2 Template D, for the appliqué border
30 Template F, for the appliqué border
From the green print, cut:
½"-wide bias strips to total 100" for stems
From the dark yellow print, cut:
8 Template E

TIP

Keep a small tin handy for your flower pieces. Add matching thread, embroidery floss, scissors, and a needle. Keep the tin with your quilt so you can appliqué whenever you have a free moment.

Construction

All seam allowances are ⅛" wide. Refer to "Basic Techniques" on pages 10–17 for construction methods. When stitching, be sure to use a piece of Stitch-n-Tear to stabilize the seams.

1. Using the pattern on page 85, trace 13 Fan blocks onto tracing paper with an ultra-fine permanent pen. Label each section with its appropriate number.

2. Use the remaining prints to complete 13 Fan blocks, referring to "Piecing with Paper Foundations" on pages 12–13 and the photo on page 30. Trim the blocks on all sides, leaving a ⅛"-wide seam allowance. Leave the tracing paper attached as a sewing guide.

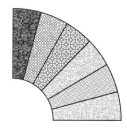

3. Cut a piece of Sulky Solvy a little larger than the unfinished fan. Place it right sides together with the fan and stitch on the seam line along the top and bottom arcs. Remove the tracing paper and turn the fan right side out.

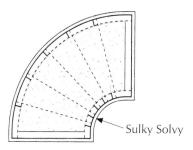

Sulky Solvy

4. Press the fan on the fabric side. Do not press on the Sulky Solvy; it will melt onto your iron.

5. Position 1 fan on each 2¾" light solid square as shown. Appliqué the top arc of the fan with a buttonhole stitch, adding a bead at each seam intersection if desired. Blindstitch the bottom arc to the background.

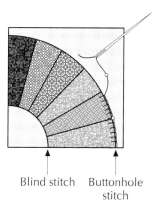

Blind stitch   Buttonhole stitch

6. Dip the blocks in water to dissolve the Sulky Solvy, and carefully lay them out to dry.

7. Embellish the fans with lace and beads as desired. Refer to the photo on page 30.

Assembly

1. Arrange the blocks and setting triangles as shown. Sew the blocks together in rows, then sew the rows together. Add the corner triangles last.

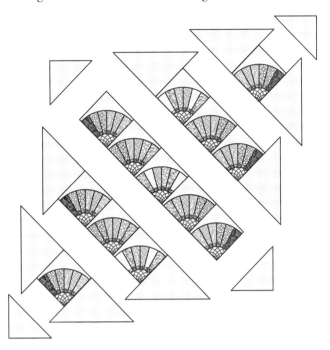

2. Arrange 2 light solid ⅞" x 15" strips with the ⅝" x 15" dark blue strip; offset the strips as shown, and sew them together along the long edge. Repeat with the ⅞" x 9" light solid strips and the ⅝" x 9" print strips. Make a total of 4 strip sets.

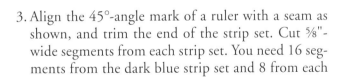

3. Align the 45°-angle mark of a ruler with a seam as shown, and trim the end of the strip set. Cut ⅝"-wide segments from each strip set. You need 16 segments from the dark blue strip set and 8 from each of the remaining sets.

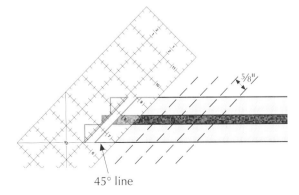

5/8"

45° line

Cut 16 dark blue.
Cut 8 each medium blue, rose, and purple.

4. To make a diamond border, arrange 10 segments, offsetting them as shown, and sew them together. Place 1 dark blue segment at each end and 2 in the middle; alternate the remaining colors between the dark blue segments. Add a background strip to each end. Make 4 diamond borders.

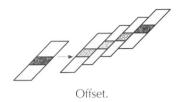

Offset.

5. Trim each side of the border strips, including the ends, leaving ⅛"-wide seam allowances. The strips should be ¾" wide.

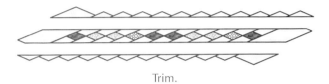

Trim.

6. Measure the length of the diamond border, including the seam allowances. Trim the quilt top to match these measurements.

Trim quilt top to match border measurements.

7. Using the pattern on page 85, trace 4 corner squares onto tracing paper with a black ultra-fine permanent marker. Label as indicated. Using the light solid and light rose fabrics, construct 4 blocks.

Make 4.

8. Sew the corner squares to opposite ends of 2 diamond borders. Referring to "Borders with Corner Squares" on pages 77–78, sew the borders to the quilt top, first to the top and bottom edges and then to the sides.

9. Referring to "Borders with Mitered Corners" on pages 78–79, measure the quilt top; cut the 2½"-wide light solid strips to fit, then add them to the quilt top.

Appliqué

This is an optional border for the truly fanatical miniature-quilt artist. Use the templates on pages 84–85.

1. From freezer paper, cut 64 Leaf Template A and 24 Leaf Template B.
2. Press the freezer-paper templates to the right side of the green print and cut them out, adding ³⁄₁₆"-wide seam allowances.

3. Using the placement guide on page 84, trace the stems and leaves onto the border.
4. Referring to "Appliquéing with Freezer Paper" on pages 16–17, appliqué the stems first, then the leaves.
5. To make the Yo-yo flowers, turn under ⅛" along the raw edge of each circle C and baste with a running stitch. Pull the threads to gather the circle, and tie a knot to hold it. Hide the thread inside the Yo-yo.

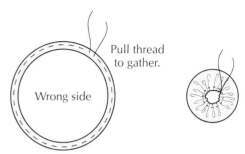

Pull thread to gather.

Wrong side

6. Referring to the placement guide, appliqué the Yo-yos onto the leaves to form clusters. Stitch a seed bead in the center of each Yo-yo.

7. For the spring blossoms, turn under ⅛" along the raw edge of each circle D. Place a yellow circle E in the center of each circle D, then pull the thread to gather the circle. A dab of glue will hold circle E in place.

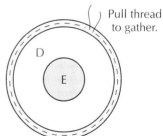
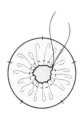

Pull thread to gather.

D
E

8. Using the marking template on page 84, make 5 marks on the Yo-yo. To form the blossom, prepare a needle with thread that matches the Yo-yo. Insert the needle from the back of the Yo-yo, then pull it through the center and around to the back again, placing the thread loop on the mark. Pull the thread snug to draw in the edge. Repeat on the 4 remaining marks. Appliqué the blossoms in place, referring to the placement guide. Stitch 3 seed beads in the center of each blossom.

Spring Blossom
Make 8.

9. To make the painted daisies, fold 5 circles F into quarters, right sides out. Baste along the lower raw edge of 1 petal, through all layers; add another petal on the same thread, basting along the lower edge through all layers. Repeat until you have 5 petals on the thread. Make sure the folds are on the same side.

Fold circle into quarters.

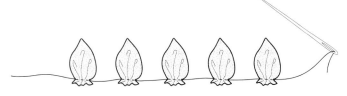

10. Draw the thread ends together, gathering the petals into a circle. Tie a knot. Sew the petals in place on the border, stitching along the gathered edge of the petals. Tack the points in place. Make 12 Yo-yos from

the rose circles G. Do not turn under the raw edge. With the smooth side up, appliqué the Yo-yo to the petals, covering the raw edges. Attach a seed bead at the center of each Yo-yo.

Tie ends together   Stitch the petals
to form a circle.   in place.

Painted Daisy
Make 12.

11. To construct the forget-me-nots, place two 1" blue squares right sides together. Using a ⅛"-wide seam allowance, stitch 3 sides together, leaving one side open for turning. Turn the squares right side out. Turn the raw edges of the opening to the inside. Using a fabric gluestick, glue the opening closed.

TIP

Turning these squares can be tricky. I place a chopstick on the seam opposite the opening and push it through the opening, then I use the chopstick to push out the corners.

12. Using matching thread and working from the back of the square, insert the needle ¼" from the center of the square, toward the middle of one side. Bring the thread around the edge and to the back of the square, drawing in the edge. Repeat on the 3 remaining sides.

13. Using contrasting embroidery thread and a straight stitch, embroider the middle design. Attach a seed bead to the center. Appliqué the forget-me-nots to the border, tacking down each corner.

Forget-Me-Not
Make 12.

Finishing

1. Layer the quilt top with batting and backing; baste.
2. Quilt as desired, or follow the quilting suggestion.

Quilting Suggestion

3. Bind the edges of the quilt. Referring to "Labeling Your Quilt" on page 81, add a label.

Potential Problems and How to Solve Them

"The ends of the fan arcs turn in."

Use a seam ripper to pull the edges out when you iron and also when you pin the fan to the background.

"The Yo-yos won't gather tightly into a circle."

Vary the length of the running stitch.

"The inner-border diamonds are vertical instead of horizontal."

Rotate the diamond strips 90° so the diamonds are horizontal.

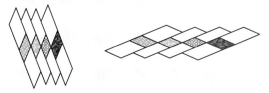

"The diamond border is too long."

Take a thread's width more on each seam allowance. After you do a few seams, check the fit against the quilt top. Hang in there; it's worth it in the end.

TIP

To calculate the size square to cut for side-setting triangles, measure the diagonal length of the finished block and add 1". Cut a square to this size, then cut the square twice diagonally for 4 side setting triangles. Cut the corner triangles from squares the same size as your finished block.

Tulips-Go-Round

QUILT SIZE: 14¼" x 14¼"

BLOCK SIZE: 3"

SKILL LEVEL: ADVANCED

COLOR PHOTO: PAGE 18

TECHNIQUES:
Appliquéing with Freezer Paper
Making Tiny Stems

Materials: 44"-wide fabric

½ yd. light solid for background,
outer border, and binding

¼ yd. red stripe for tulips
and inner border

¼ yd. green solid for leaves and stems

⅛ yd. red solid for tulip centers

16" x 16" piece for backing

16" x 16" piece of batting

Cutting

From the light solid, cut:

1 square, 9" x 9", for the appliqué block (The square is cut larger
than needed; trim it after the appliqué is complete.)

2 strips, each 2½" x 42", for the outer border

From the red stripe, cut:

1 strip, ½" x 38", for the inner border

From the green solid, cut:

½"-wide bias strips to total 80" for stems

Appliqué

1. Apply FrayCheck along the edges of the light solid square. To
guide placement of the appliqué pieces, use a pencil to lightly
mark each side of the square 1" from the edge. Fold the square in
half, then fold it again to the mark. Lightly press to crease the
edges. Repeat in the opposite direction.

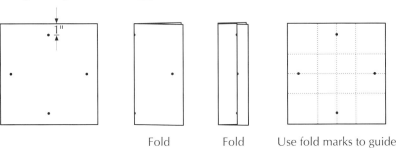

Fold
in half.

Fold
to mark.

Use fold marks to guide
block placement.

2. Referring to the placement guide on page 85, mark the placement of the stems on the light solid block with a washable marker. Use the creases as a guide.
3. Referring to "Appliquéing Tiny Stems" on page 17, appliqué the ½"-wide green bias strips in place.
4. Using the patterns on page 85, trace 20 each of Templates A, B, C, and D onto the dull (uncoated) side of freezer paper. Cut out the templates and iron them onto the right side of the appropriate fabric. Refer to "Appliquéing with Freezer Paper" on pages 16–17.
5. Referring to the placement guide, appliqué the leaves in place, then the tulips. Stitch the tulip centers first. Use a gluestick to position the small pieces.

Assembly and Finishing

All seam allowances are ⅛" wide. Refer to "Basic Techniques" on pages 10–17 for construction methods. When stitching, be sure to use a piece of Stitch-n-Tear to stabilize the seams.
1. Trim the appliqué block to 8¼" x 8¼".
2. Referring to "Borders with Straight-Cut Corners" on page 77, measure the quilt top. From the ½"-wide red-stripe strips, cut 2 borders to fit the top and bottom edges; sew them to the quilt top. Cut 2 borders to fit the side edges; add them to the quilt top. Add the outer borders in the same manner.

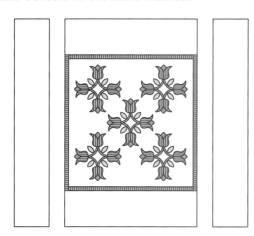

3. Referring to the placement guide on page 85, prepare and appliqué border stems, leaves, and tulips.
4. Layer the quilt top with batting and backing; baste.

5. Quilt as desired, or follow the quilting suggestion.

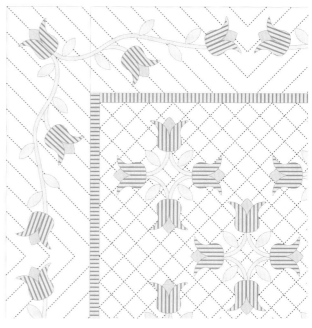

Quilting Suggestion

6. Bind the edges of the quilt. Referring to "Labeling Your Quilt" on page 81, add a label.

Potential Problems and How to Solve Them

"The stem puckers on the inside curve."

Make sure the stem is cut on the bias grain of the fabric and is first stitched to the inside of the curve.

"The green thread on my quilt bled."

Test your thread as well as your fabric for colorfastness before using them in your quilt.

Yo-Yo's Garden

QUILT SIZE: 18" x 18"
BLOCK SIZE: 3"
SKILL LEVEL: ADVANCED
COLOR PHOTO: PAGE 28
TECHNIQUES:
Appliquéing Curves
Constructing Yo-Yos
Making an Ice-Cream Cone Border
Finishing a Scalloped Edge

Materials: 44"-wide fabric

½ yd. light solid for
background and borders

⅛ yd. green print for
stems and leaves

⅛ yd. pink print for Yo-yo flowers

⅛ yd. yellow solid for Yo-yo insets

1 yd. blue plaid for blocks,
borders, and facing

15½" x 15½" piece for backing

19" x 19" piece of batting

Cutting

Use the templates on page 86.
From the light solid, cut:
13 squares, each 3¼" x 3¼"
2 squares, each 5½" x 5½"; cut each square twice
diagonally for 8 side setting triangles
2 squares, each 3¼" x 3¼";
cut each square once diagonally for 4 corner triangles
From the green print, cut:
2 strips, each ½" x 42", for stems
From the pink print, cut:
48 Template C
From the yellow solid, cut:
48 Template D
From the blue plaid, cut:
2 strips, each ⅝" x 42", for the inner border
1 square, 19" x 19", for the facing

Construction

All seam allowances are ⅛" wide. Refer to "Basic Techniques" on pages 10–17 for construction methods. When stitching, be sure to use a piece of Stitch-n-Tear to stabilize the seams. Use the templates on page 86.

1. From freezer paper, cut 36 Template A. Iron the templates to the right side of the remaining blue plaid. Cut them out, adding a ³⁄₁₆"-wide seam allowance along the curved edge and a ⅛"-wide seam allowance along the straight edges.

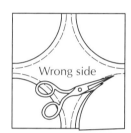

2. Place 1 piece A in each corner of the light solid square and appliqué the curved edge. Trim the background fabric behind each piece A, leaving a ⅛"-wide seam allowance.

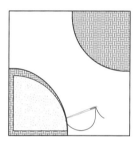

3. Fold each 3¼" light solid square in half and crease. Fold in half again and crease. Fold the side setting and corner triangles as shown and crease. The creases are your placement guidelines.

| Background Square | Side Setting Triangle | Corner Triangle |

4. Cut the ½"-wide green strip into 36 pieces, each ¾" long, and arrange them on the crease lines of the 3¼" light solid squares, side setting triangles, and corner triangles as shown. Appliqué them in place, referring to "Appliquéing Tiny Stems" on page 17.

5. From freezer paper, cut 96 Template B. Iron the freezer-paper templates to the right side of the remaining green print; cut out the leaves, adding a ³⁄₁₆"-wide seam allowance. Appliqué 2 leaves to each stem as shown.

6. Center a yellow circle D on the wrong side of each pink circle C. (Dab circle D with a gluestick to hold it in place.) Referring to step 7 of "Fan-itsies" on page 65, make 48 Yo-yos with yellow inserts.

7. Appliqué a Yo-yo to the top of each stem.

Assembly

1. Arrange the blocks, side setting triangles, and corner triangles as shown in the quilt plan on page 70. Sew the blocks and triangles together in rows, pressing the seams in opposite directions from row to row. Join the rows.

2. Referring to "Borders with Mitered Corners" on pages 78–79, measure the quilt top for borders. Trim the ⅝"-wide inner border strips to fit and sew them to the quilt top, mitering the corners.

3. From freezer paper, cut 40 Template E, 4 Template F, and 36 Template G. Iron Templates E and F onto the wrong side of the remaining blue plaid; iron Template G to the wrong side of the remaining light solid. Cut out the pieces, adding a ⅛"-wide seam allowance all around.

4. Referring to "Piecing with Freezer-Paper Templates" on pages 11–12, assemble 4 Ice-Cream Cone borders. Begin piecing with piece E, then add piece G. Alternate pieces E and G, ending with piece E. Do not remove the freezer paper.

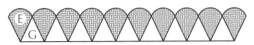

Make 4.

5. Sew 2 borders to opposite side edges of the quilt top; start and stop the stitching ⅛" from each end.

6. Add 1 piece F to each end of the 2 remaining borders. Stitch the borders to the top and bottom edges of the quilt top; start and stop ⅛" from each end.

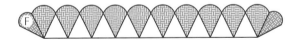

7. To sew piece F to piece E, stitch from the inside corner toward the outside edge; use the freezer paper as a stitching guide.

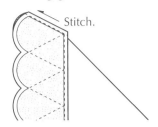

Stitch.

Finishing

1. Cut a 12½" x 12½" square from the center of the 19" x 19" blue plaid square. This is the facing.

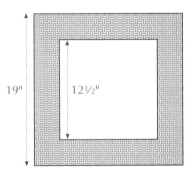

19"   12½"

2. Place the facing on the quilt top, right sides together. Stitch the quilt top to the facing, using the freezer paper as a stitching guide. Trim the excess facing, following the scalloped edge.

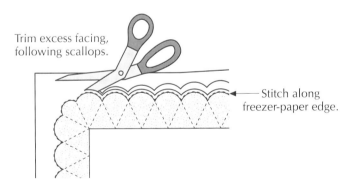

Trim excess facing, following scallops.

Stitch along freezer-paper edge.

3. Turn the facing to the back; then turn under the raw edges, clipping the corners as necessary.

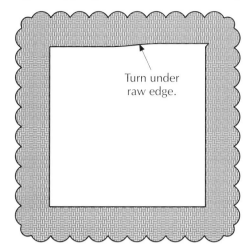

Turn under raw edge.

4. Place the quilt top on the batting; cut the batting to match the quilt top, following the scalloped edges.

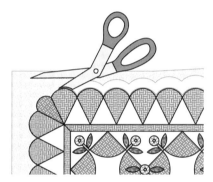

Cut batting to fit quilt top.

5. Slip the batting inside the facing. Insert the backing, right side up, on top of the batting and under the facing.

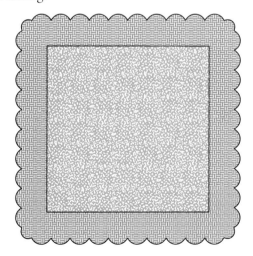

6. Baste the center of the quilt up to the facing. Quilt this area first, then blindstitch the facing to the inner border. (This helps eliminate puckering.) Once the facing is blindstitched in place, quilt the border.

7. Quilt as desired, or follow the quilting suggestion.

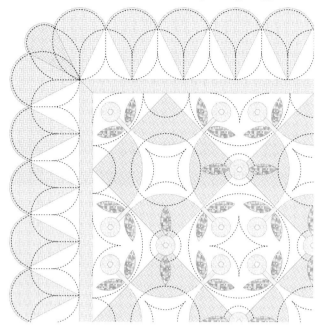

Quilting Suggestion

8. Referring to "Labeling Your Quilt" on page 81, add a label.

Potential Problems and How to Solve Them

"The Yo-yos won't gather into tight circles."

Vary the length of the running stitches.

"The Yo-yos were too small to pin in place without distorting."

Add a dab of fabric glue and set them in place for stitching. Try this with the leaves too.

Blackjack

QUIT SIZE: 15" x 15"
BLOCK SIZE: 2½"
SKILL LEVEL: ADVANCED
COLOR PHOTO: PAGE 31
TECHNIQUES:
Piecing with Paper Foundations
Piecing with Freezer-Paper Templates
Using ¼"-Wide Seam Allowances
on the Block Perimeter

Materials: 44"-wide fabric

½ yd. light solid for background

½ yd. *total* assorted black prints for blocks, border, and binding

¼ yd. purple print for blocks

¼ yd. blue-violet print for blocks

16" x 16" piece for backing

16" x 16" piece of batting

Construction

Seam allowances vary from ⅛" to ¼" wide, depending on the section of the quilt you are working on. When stitching, use a piece of Stitch-n-Tear to stabilize the seams.

1. Using the pattern on page 76, trace 80 star foundations onto tracing paper and label the piecing sequence. The foundation is drafted so the outer edge of the block has a ¼"-wide seam allowance, which makes it easier to match points.

2. Referring to "Piecing with Paper Foundations" on pages 12–13, construct 48 star sections with the purple print and 32 with the blue-violet print for the star points. Use the light solid for the background sections.

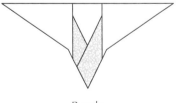

Purple
Make 48.

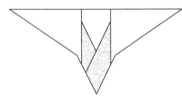

Blue-Violet
Make 32.

3. Cut 80 Template A from freezer paper and iron the templates to the wrong side of the assorted black prints. Cut out the fabric pieces, adding ⅛"-wide seam allowances.

4. Working from the center as shown, stitch a black piece to the star section, starting and stopping ⅛" from each end. Do not stitch into the seam allowance.

Begin and end stitching at the seam intersections.

5. Assemble the blocks as shown.

Make 8 purple.   Make 12 blue-violet.

Assembly and Finishing

1. Referring to the photo on page 31, arrange the blocks in 4 rows of 4 blocks each. Reserve 4 blue-violet blocks for the border. Using a ¼"-wide seam allowance, sew the blocks into rows, then join the rows.

2. Using the border foundations on page 76, trace 4 section #1, 20 section #2, and 4 section #3. Label the piecing sequence of each foundation.

NOTE: *The outer edges have ¼"-wide seam allowances. Refer to the foundation templates when trimming the seam allowances.*

3. Arrange 1 section #1 foundation, 5 section #2 foundations, and 1 section #3 foundation as shown. Label the colors on each foundation, then construct the sections. Assemble each section, then join the sections as shown to form a border.

4. Using a ¼"-wide seam allowance, sew 2 borders to opposite side edges of the quilt top.

5. Add a Star block to each end of the remaining border strips, then stitch the borders to the top and bottom edges.

  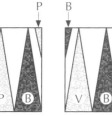    

Section #1   Section #2   Section #2   Section #2   Section #2   Section #2   Section #3

B = Black   P = Purple   V = Blue-violet

Make 4.

6. Layer the quilt top with batting and backing; baste.
7. Quilt as desired, or follow the quilting suggestion.

Quilting Suggestion

8. Trim the outer edges to ⅛" from the points.
9. Bind the edges of the quilt. Referring to "Labeling Your Quilt" on page 81, add a label.

Potential Problems and How to Solve Them

"I'm having a hard time sewing piece A."

Make sure the freezer paper is firmly adhered; if it isn't, the bias edge will stretch. Treat this as an inset seam; do not stitch into the seam allowance at the inside point.

Blackjack
Template and Foundations

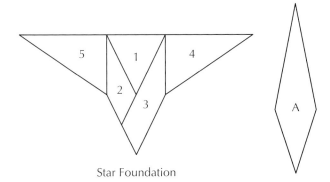

Star Foundation

Inside edge: ⅛" seam allowance

Border Foundations

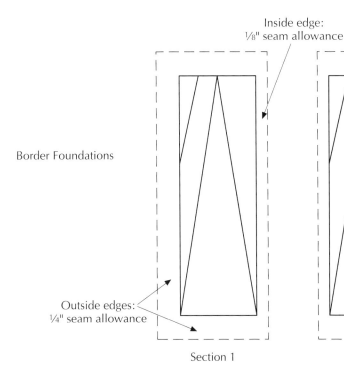

Outside edges: ¼" seam allowance

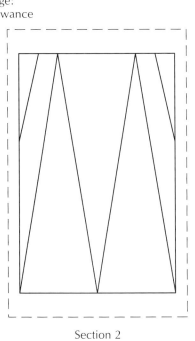

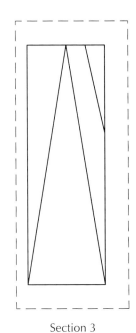

Section 1

Section 2

Section 3

FINISHING TECHNIQUES

ADDING BORDERS

The border can make or break a quilt and can take your miniature quilt from pot holder status to work of art. The border should contain and enhance the main design without overpowering it. Some quilts call for a straight border while others cry out for pieced, scalloped, or even appliquéd borders. I often wait until the main body of the quilt is finished before I plan the border, then I let the central design dictate the next step. Repeating elements of the quilt design in the border preserves the integrity of the quilt. Other times I find a fabric that is particularly appropriate for a border, and I design a quilt specifically for that piece of fabric.

Borders with Straight-Cut Corners

I prefer to add the top and bottom borders first because doing so visually lengthens the quilt; adding top and bottom borders last seems to visually stunt a quilt.

1. Measure the width of the quilt top through the center. Trim 2 border strips to this measurement.

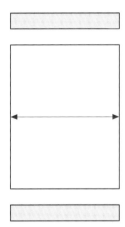

2. Sew the border strips to the top and bottom edges of the quilt top, easing the quilt top to fit if necessary. (By fitting the borders to the center measurement, the quilt stays square and lies flat.) Press the seams toward the border strips.

3. Measure the length of the quilt top through the center, including the top and bottom borders. Cut 2 border strips to this measurement

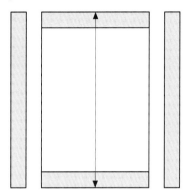

4. Sew the border strips to the side edges of the quilt top, easing the quilt top to fit if necessary.
5. If there is more than one border, repeat the process.

Borders with Corner Squares

Add little surprises to the corner squares. Use a different color as an accent or include a fussy-cut flower or geometric design.

1. Measure the length and width of the quilt top through the center. Cut 2 top and bottom borders and 2 side borders to these measurements.

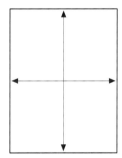

2. Sew the side borders to the quilt top.

3. Sew the corner squares to each end of the top and bottom strips, then sew the borders to the quilt top.

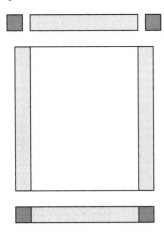

Borders with Mitered Corners

Mitered borders can be intimidating until you try them.

1. Measure the length and width of the quilt top through the center. Add double the width of the border to these measurements, then add an extra 1" for seam allowances and matching. Cut the border strips to these measurements.

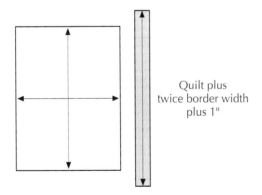

Quilt plus
twice border width
plus 1"

2. If you are adding multiple borders, sew them together into one strip before attaching them to the quilt top; then treat the borders as one piece of fabric.

Treat the joined fabrics as one.

3. Sew each border to the quilt top, starting and stopping ⅛" from each end; backstitch.

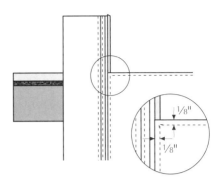

4. Place the quilt right side up on an ironing board. Lay one border strip flat. Fold the adjacent border strip under at a 45° angle, aligning it, right sides together, with the other strip.

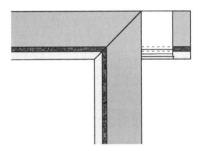

5. If there are multiple borders, make sure they align. Press a crease in the fold, then place a piece of tape over the mitered corner to hold it in place.

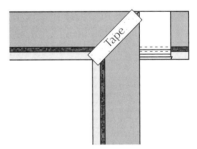

6. Fold the quilt top diagonally, right sides together, and draw a line on the border along the crease.

7. Stitch on the marked line and remove the tape. Trim the excess fabric and press the seam open.

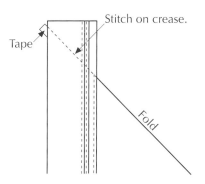

Tape

Stitch on crease.

Fold

USING BATTING AND BACKING

There are a number of battings that work well for miniature quilts. Fairfield Cotton Classic™ works if you peel it into two layers, iron the fuzzies down, and face them toward the backing. Fairfield Soft Touch®, a wonderful 100% cotton batting, is my favorite. It requires no peeling and is thin enough even for micro-mini quilts. I don't use polyester battings in my quilts, but a lot of people have success with Hobbs Thermore®.

Treat the backing as an added surprise. Those jazzy, snazzy, funky prints that are a statement in themselves make wonderful backings. I prefer not to piece the backing of a miniature quilt. I like to quilt my miniatures extensively, and the added bulk of a pieced back makes quilting difficult.

BASTING YOUR MINIATURE

Because most miniatures are not quilted in a hoop, basting is essential. Press the backing, smooth it out on a hard surface, right side down, and tape the edges to the surface; start in the middle and work toward the corners, adding masking tape every few inches.

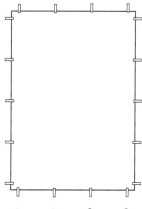

Place the batting on the backing, then center and smooth the quilt top over the batting, right side up. Baste a grid every 1½", starting from the center. When the grid is complete, baste around the outside edge.

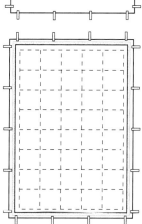

QUILTING YOUR MINIATURE

One of the most satisfying aspects of quilting is watching the quilt come alive. The secondary design created by the quilting breathes life into the quilt. I love to watch the transformation from a flat, lifeless surface to one that has dimension and soul.

I begin quilting with a general design in mind, but as I quilt, the design begins to take shape almost on its own. The pieced shapes tend to dictate the design. Incorporating the pieced design into the quilting design gives the quilt an overall unity.

Plan your quilting design as if it were for a full-size quilt. Scale the design to fit the miniature so it is a complete representation of a full-size quilting design. This final effort raises your piece to a work of art. There is a piece of your life and soul in every stitch you put into your quilt, and it shows in the quilting.

Follow the path of least resistance when quilting a miniature. Plan a design that avoids the seams as much as possible. As you scaled down the pieced design, scale down the quilting as well.

Use a thread weight that is appropriate to the size of the quilt. I use 100% cotton quilting thread, but I try to find thread that is a finer weight. Coating thread with beeswax helps keep it from fraying and tangling. Don't be afraid to use colored quilting threads to add a little interest.

I have never used a hoop to quilt a miniature quilt. The absence of a hoop demands a different needling technique: place the fabric on the needle rather than running the needle through the fabric. If you want to quilt your miniature in a hoop, attach an edging to make it large enough to accommodate one.

TIP

I wear a .025 metal guitar pick on the finger underneath the quilt. Picks are available at music stores and are inexpensive. For added comfort, wear it over a rubber finger, which also protects your fingernail.

When quilting micro-minis, I use a special technique that I call decorative quilting. With this technique, the quilt appears to be fully quilted on the top but is actually only tacked through to the back in certain spots. Even with ⅛"-wide seam allowances, when the full quilt size is only 4" x 5", the main design has too much seam bulk for straight quilting. With decorative quilting, I use a quilting stitch through the top layer only. In the center of a square, where there is no seam bulk, I tack through to the back. Plan the quilting design beforehand so the tacking will be uniform.

With the decorative-quilting method, all three layers are joined and the quilting design is to scale. I know this method is cheating, but with minis we can break the rules! Quilt the border of a micro-mini quilt in the traditional fashion.

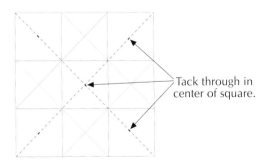

Tack through in center of square.

Back view of quilting

BINDING THE EDGES

For a miniature quilt, it isn't necessary to cut the binding on the bias. There will be no wear or tear on these little quilts. The exceptions are quilts with curved edges or scalloped borders, such as "Morning Glory" (page 56).

For interest, use several different-colored strips stitched together in various lengths. (See "Spools" on page 25.) Use a fabric other than the border fabric to add interest to scrappy quilts.

NOTE: Use the border fabric to bind micro-mini quilts. A contrasting binding can work with a miniature quilt, but it overpowers a tiny one. Cut the binding strip ¾" wide, and use a scant ⅛"-wide seam allowance when stitching it to the quilt.

1. Cut the binding strips 1⅛"-wide. This will give you a ⅛"-wide finished binding. Join the binding strips, wrong sides together, with a diagonal seam. Fold the binding in half lengthwise, wrong sides together, and press.

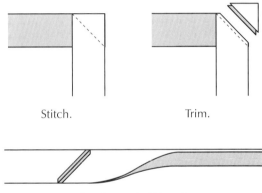

Stitch.   Trim.

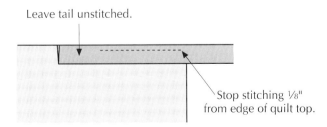

Press binding in half lengthwise.

2. Align the raw edges of the binding with the raw edges of the quilt. Begin stitching approximately ⅓ of the distance from the corner on the bottom edge. Stitch, leaving a 3" tail and using a ⅛"-wide seam allowance. Stop stitching ⅛" from the edge.

Leave tail unstitched.

Stop stitching ⅛" from edge of quilt top.

3. Fold the binding straight up, away from the quilt, forming a 45°-angle fold. Bring the binding straight down, aligning it with the next edge. (The top fold should be even with the first edge of the quilt.) Begin stitching at the edge, sewing through all layers. Continue to the next corner and repeat.

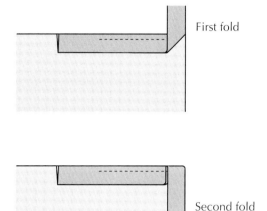

First fold

Second fold

4. Continue around the quilt, leaving a 3" tail at the end. Overlap the ends by the width of the binding. (For example, if the binding was cut 1⅛"-wide, overlap the ends by 1⅛".) Trim the excess.

Overlap original
cut width of binding.

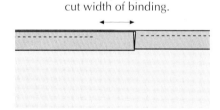

5. Unfold the binding. Lay the ends right sides together, at right angles to each other, with the right end on top of the left. Draw a diagonal line from the upper left corner to the lower right. Pin and stitch.

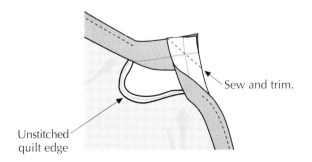

Sew and trim.

Unstitched
quilt edge

6. Trim the edge and press the seam open. Refold the binding in half and finish stitching. It will fit perfectly!

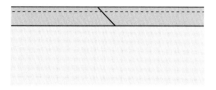

Refold and stitch.

7. Turn the binding to the back and blind stitch. Fold the miters on the back as you come to them.

LABELING YOUR QUILT

The easiest way I have found to create labels for my quilts is to use a variety of rubber stamps and a permanent ink pad. There are many rubber stamps to choose from, and the ink pad can be purchased at any office-supply store.

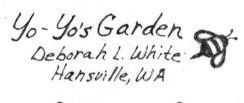

1. Cut a piece of freezer paper 2" x 3" and iron it to the back of a 3" x 4" piece of muslin. This creates a stable surface for stamping and writing.
2. Ink the stamp on the stamp pad and stamp the muslin. This creates a black outline which can be filled in with colored permanent pens. (You can use colored stamp pads if they have permanent ink.)
3. Sign your name and the date with a permanent pen, and include other information as desired.
4. Turn the edges to the back over the freezer paper and press to crease it and to set the ink.
5. Remove the freezer paper and stitch the label to the back of your miniature treasure.

TEMPLATES AND FOUNDATIONS

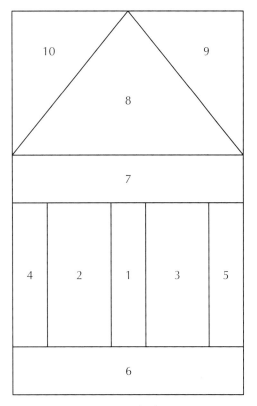

House Block

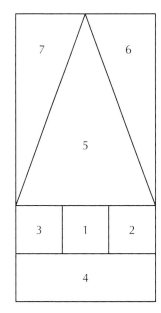

Tree #1

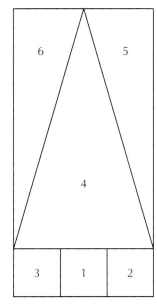

Tree #2

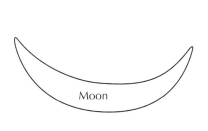

Moon

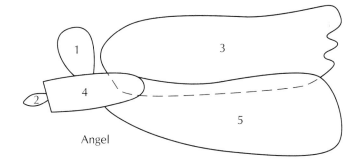

Angel

Angel to Watch Over Me
Templates and Foundations

Morning Glory
Templates and Foundation

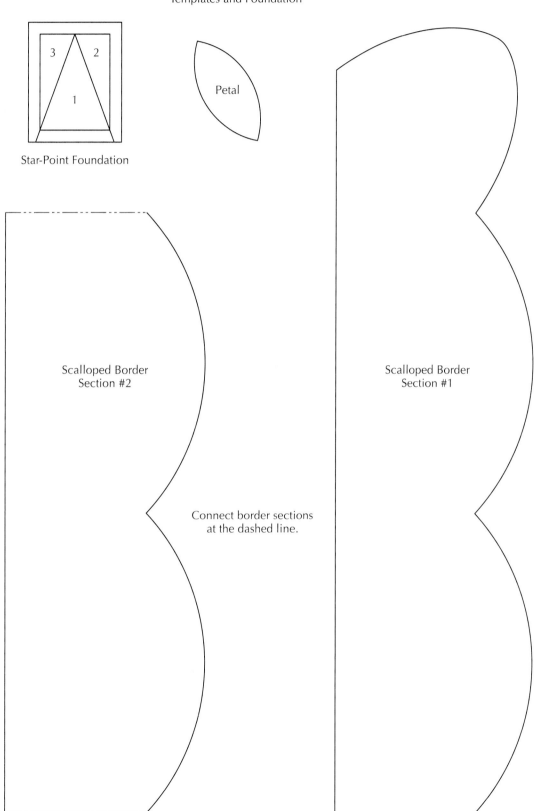

3 2

1

Star-Point Foundation

Petal

Scalloped Border
Section #2

Scalloped Border
Section #1

Connect border sections
at the dashed line.

Fan-Itsies
Templates and Placement Guide

G

E

C

D

Marking
Template

F

Join sections
at right angles.

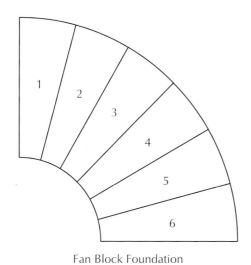

Fan Block Foundation

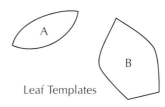

Leaf Templates

Corner Square Foundation

Tulips-Go-Round
Templates, Placement Guides,
and Border Pattern

Yo-Yo's Garden
Templates and Placement Guide

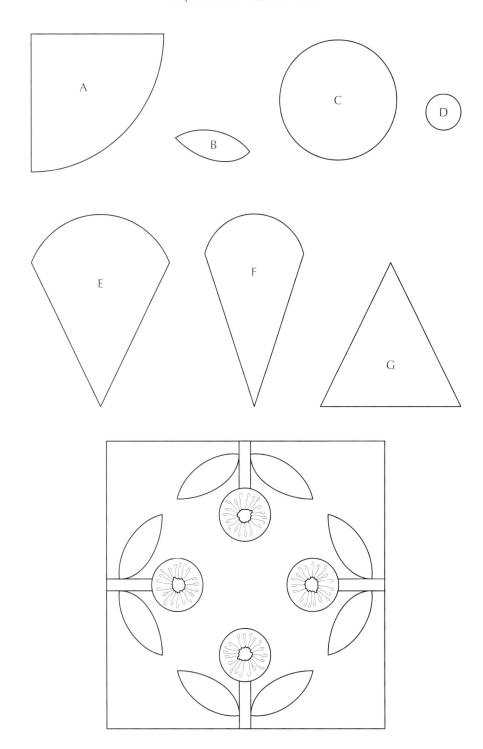

A

B

C

D

E

F

G

Technique Index

About the Author

Debbie White was introduced to needlework at the age of nine by her grandmother, who taught her to knit and crochet. Later, when she learned embroidery, that became her creative outlet. Quilting caught Debbie's interest in 1982. The love of quilting progressed into a passion for miniature quilts, which have become the focus of Debbie's love of intricate handwork. The need for a challenge carried Debbie into local and national competition, and she has won numerous awards for her miniature quilts.

A native of Washington state, Debbie lives with her husband and three children in the town of Hansville. She teaches and lectures at local quilt shops and guilds and is a member of the Kitsap Quilters.

Publications and Products